— American Forces in Berlin —

1945–1994

Cold War Outpost

♦

by
Robert P. Grathwol
Donita M. Moorhus

Department of Defense
Legacy Resource Management Program
Cold War Project
Washington, D.C.
1994

Library of Congress Cataloging-in-Publication Data

Grathwol, Robert P., 1939–
       American forces in Berlin : Cold War outpost, 1945–1994 / by
Robert P. Grathwol, Donita M. Moorhus.
             p. cm.
       Includes bibliographical references and index.
       1. Berlin (Germany)—History—1945–1990.   2. United States—Armed
Forces—Germany—Berlin.   3. Berlin (Germany)—History—Blockade,
1948–1949.   4. United States—Military relations—Germany.
5. Germany—Military relations—United States.   I. Moorhus, Donita
M., 1942–   . II. Title.
DD881.G63 1994
943.1'554'087—dc20   94-32631
                                                                          CIP

Notes on the Cover

The front cover is a montage of photographs of the Brandenburg Gate, representing the transition of Berlin
from division to reunification. The back cover is a photograph of graffiti on the Berlin Wall.

For sale by the U.S. Government Printing Office
Superintendent of Documents, Mail Stop: SSOP, Washington, DC 20402-9328
ISBN 0-16-045272-4

Contents

Legacy Program

Established by Congress in 1991, the Legacy Resource Management Program promotes the responsible stewardship of cultural, historical, and natural resources on Department of Defense lands, seeking to integrate the conservation of these irreplaceable resources with the missions of the military service.

The Cold War Project is one of nine directives outlined in the legislation authorizing the Legacy Program. The project strives to inventory, protect, and conserve the Defense Department's physical and literary property and artifacts at home and abroad that relate to the origins and development of the Cold War. Because the Cold War is less than fifty years old, the significance of much of the material culture from the period is yet to be determined. And because much of the property overseas has been or will be returned to host nations, it cannot be preserved according to American standards.

The Cold War Project promotes the preservation of our nation's cultural and historical legacy through a variety of activities, including this book. With this and other studies and research efforts, the Cold War Project helps conserve the record of the Department of Defense's roles and contributions during a critical period in recent history and makes that record available to the public.

Foreword

When the United States flag over Berlin was furled on September 8, 1994, it ended almost half a century of U.S. and allied occupation of West Berlin. The U.S. garrison in the city was the guarantor of our firm resolution that West Berlin would remain free. In isolated West Berlin, surrounded by Communist East Germany, East and West confronted each other during the Berlin Airlift in 1948–49 and then across the thickets of barbed wire and the ugly concrete of the Berlin Wall erected in 1961.

The Berlin Wall lasted from 1961 to 1989—more than 28 years. It did not break the spirit of the Berliners or diminish the resolution of the United States and its allies to guarantee the freedom of West Berlin. The world watched in awe and then celebrated as citizens of a divided Germany reduced the Wall to rubble in November 1989. The end of the Communist regime in East Germany permitted the reunification of Germany and Berlin. When the dissolution of the Soviet Union followed, the Cold War between the Soviet Union and the West came to an end.

This illustrated history of American forces in Berlin depicts people, places, and events that occurred in that vital and furthest U.S. outpost in Central Europe during the Cold War. It helps thus to preserve the invaluable legacy of the U.S. military's contribution to the fulfillment of the American commitment to freedom and democracy.

WILLIAM J. PERRY
Secretary of Defense

The Authors

Robert P. Grathwol

Robert P. Grathwol is a historian, researcher, and writer. For over 20 years as a university professor, he taught twentieth century European and German history. Since 1988, he has concentrated his research and writing on studies of the Cold War, particularly the activities of the American military in Europe from 1945 to 1991. In 1992, he completed a major study for the U.S. Army Corps of Engineers on military construction in Europe during the Cold War. He is the author of *Stresemann and the DNVP* (Lawrence: The Regents Press of Kansas, 1980) as well as articles and reviews in scholarly journals both in English and German. A former Fulbright Scholar to France and a Humboldt Fellow to Germany, Dr. Grathwol has a B.A. from Providence College, a Diplôme Supérieur from the University of Strasbourg, France, and a Ph.D. from the University of Chicago.

Donita M. Moorhus

Donita M. Moorhus is an oral historian, researcher, and writer. Since 1988, she has conducted topical and full-life interviews with a wide range of individuals, including active duty and retired officers of the U.S. military, high-ranking civilian employees of the U.S. government, business and community leaders, foreign nationals, and journalists. She is co-author with Dr. Grathwol of the study of military construction in Europe during the Cold War. As managing partner of R&D Associates, Ms. Moorhus serves as the project manager for historical research and is a consultant on oral history projects. She has a B.A. from the University of Michigan and an M.S. from Fordham University.

Acknowledgments

This project is a product of cooperation. Active and retired military personnel, Berliners, Army and Air Force historians, private citizens, government officials, and contractors worked together to meet the deadlines.

As head of the Cold War Project, Department of Defense Legacy Resource Management Program, Rebecca Hancock Cameron, Center for Air Force History, conceived this project and saw it to completion.

William C. Baldwin, U.S. Army Corps of Engineers, Office of History, coordinated the players, monitored the contracts, and encouraged all of the contractors.

Alfred Beck, Center for Air Force History, helped track down photographs, critiqued the text, and monitored the printers.

Marilyn Hunter, U.S. Army Corps of Engineers, Office of History, reviewed all the drafts, reminding us to avoid the passive and keep the sentences short.

Dana Mitchell, our designer at EEI, integrated the text, testimony, and photos, while Jayne Sutton managed the production effort.

Our research assistant, Douglas Wilson, performed a number of essential tasks, from photo research in the Library of Congress to transcribing oral history interviews to keeping the bibliography. His good eye, attention to detail, and sense of humor made him a valuable member of the team.

Historians in Germany and the United States, including Bruce Siemon, William Stivers, K. Martin Johnson, Thomas Snyder, Tom Blake, and Dan Harrington provided assistance.

We are particularly grateful to the individuals who shared their own stories, personal photographs, and memorabilia. Robert Baldinger, Klaus Bartels, James Bourk, Stephen Bowman, Lou Brettschneider, Norman Delbridge, Saul Fraint, James and Lani Graham, Lynn Hansen, Dan Lucas, Helga Mellmann, Richard Naab, Thomas Obitz, Martin Reuss, Renate Semler, Tom Starbuck, and Ken Wunsche generously helped us to understand and then to personalize the story of the American armed forces in Berlin. We acknowledge also the scores of unnamed photographers who captured and preserved images of the Americans in Berlin since 1945 for those of us who were not there.

Finally, we pay tribute to the thousands of American soldiers and airmen who risked their lives, as well as to those who lost their lives, in Berlin, outpost of freedom in the Cold War. We all owe them our gratitude.

R.P.G. and D.M.M.
Alexandria, Virginia
September 1994

Berlin from Grandeur to Defeat

World War II left Berlin shattered. In the summer of 1945, Germany's capital city lay in ruins, occupied by the armies of the United States, the Soviet Union, Great Britain, and France. The devastation of combat obscured the grandeur of Berlin's past. The city recovered, but over the next 50 years it remained an outpost for the armed forces of Germany's conquerors, a place of tension, intrigue, and conflict.

Historic Capital

Berlin's historic stature traces its beginnings to the trade routes of the Middle Ages. Early in the fourteenth century, two commercial towns on the banks of the Spree River in Eastern Europe merged to form Berlin. Over the next several centuries, the city prospered as a commercial center. By the late eighteenth century, Berlin had become a European capital city of distinction, the center of government for the powerful Prussian kings.

The city's renown increased under Frederick the Great (1740 to 1786), King of Prussia at the height of the Enlightenment era. Frederick gained a reputation for his political, military, and intellectual acumen that drew to his court a circle of

Wartime destruction in central Berlin, 1945

Brandenburg Gate in 1910

1

1200
1300
1400
1500
1600
1700
1800
1900
1910
1920
1930
1940
1941
1942
1943
1944
1945

Enlightenment philosophers, dramatists, and intellectuals. Frederick spent generously to embellish his capital. He modeled his palace-residence, Sans Souci, after French monarch Louis XIV's palace at Versailles.

Frederick's successor continued to adorn the city by commissioning the Brandenburg Gate near the heart of Berlin. Completed in the 1790s, the gate was crowned with a sculpture of a four-horse chariot bearing the goddess of victory. Over the next generation, the Brandenburg Gate became a symbol of the triumph of Germanic freedom over the oppressive imperialism of the French Revolution and Napoleon.

Berlin expanded during the nineteenth century as the administrative center of an increasingly powerful industrial Germany. By mid-century, Berlin had become a hub for overland railroad connections, with lines radiating out to the Baltic and the North Sea, to Eastern and Southeastern Europe, and to southern Germany and the Rhineland.

By 1871, Prussia had forged the first unified German state by winning a series of wars against other European powers. For the next 40 years, the new nation-state, with the Prussian king as German emperor, dominated European diplomacy; and Berlin grew as a commercial, industrial, and political center. As German might and Berlin's prestige increased, the memory of the victorious armies of the King of Prussia parading through the Brandenburg Gate turned the gate into a symbol of German power and influence.

Between World Wars

Germany descended from the apex of power at the beginning of the twentieth century into chaos in 1918. In the tumultuous era after its defeat in World War I, Germany struggled for political and economic stability. Through it all, Berlin continued to grow. It reorganized its boundaries in 1920 and expanded by incorporating 8 towns, 59 rural communities, and 27 farming estates to its present-day dimensions of 345 square miles.

During the 1920s, Berlin augmented its intellectual, artistic, and cultural reputation. The city's inhabitants supported 149 daily periodicals, earning Berlin the label "newspaper city." Nobel Prize-winning scientists lived and worked in Berlin. Walter Gropius brought the genius of his Bauhaus movement in architecture to the city. Bertolt Brecht wrote for the Berlin theater. Film and cabaret entertainment flourished, its frenetic excitement and allure captured by British author Christopher Isherwood, whose *Berlin Stories* (1946) became the basis for the Broadway musical *Cabaret*.

Adolf Hitler's appointment in January 1933 as German chancellor ended Berlin's cultural brilliance. Within months, Hitler destroyed the republican framework of German politics and suppressed intellectual independence. He despised modern artistic expression, which he labeled as a manifestation of "Jewish" decadence. His pathological hatred

Growth of Berlin

2

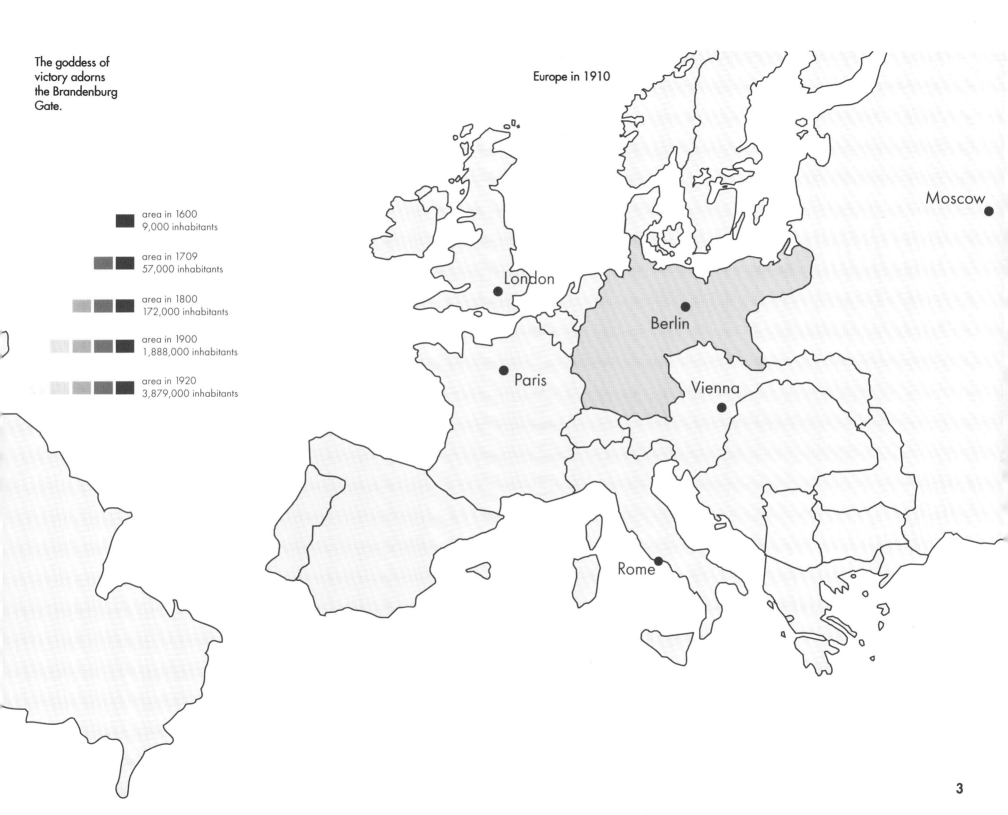

The goddess of victory adorns the Brandenburg Gate.

Europe in 1910

area in 1600
9,000 inhabitants

area in 1709
57,000 inhabitants

area in 1800
172,000 inhabitants

area in 1900
1,888,000 inhabitants

area in 1920
3,879,000 inhabitants

Moscow

London

Berlin

Paris

Vienna

Rome

3

1200
1300
1400
1500
1600
1700
1800
1900
1910
1920
1930
1940
1941
1942
1943
1944
1945

of Jews led to the organized murder of millions of men, women, and children. Of Berlin's pre-war Jewish citizenry of 170,000, over 60,000 perished in the Holocaust.

Hitler's hatred remained concealed for much of the 1930s, and Berlin remained a center of international power. Germany hosted the 1936 Olympic Games in Berlin. The city became a focal point of diplomacy as Europe stumbled again toward war. Hitler boasted that his Third Reich would last for a thousand years, and he planned to make Berlin a fitting architectural monument to a worldwide empire.

Hitler launched his bid for world empire in September 1939 by attacking Poland and touching off World War II. Within three years, his aggression had provoked a counter-coalition of world powers led by the United States, Great Britain, and the Soviet Union.

The Fall of Berlin

As the war progressed, the United States and Great Britain bombed Berlin from the air. Once engaged in Europe, however, allied commanders judged that a ground campaign to capture Berlin distracted from their principal goal: to destroy the German forces in the field.

The Soviet Union's leaders, by contrast, saw Berlin as an important strategic and psychological objective. Having driven the German invaders back from the outskirts of Moscow and Stalingrad in 1942 and 1943, the Red Army advanced to the eastern borders of Germany in 1944. The final attack on Berlin came in mid-April 1945. The Germans resisted bitterly; Soviet casualties and deaths numbered 300,000.

While the Soviets attacked Berlin from the east, American armies from the west bypassed the city and penetrated deep into Czechoslovakia in Eastern Europe. In early May 1945, with its military power shattered and its capital and country in ruins, Germany surrendered unconditionally to the allied coalition.

During the war, the United States, Great Britain, and the Soviet Union had crafted diplomatic plans to occupy postwar Germany. The agreements divided Germany into zones and Berlin into sectors, each assigned to one of the three powers. In each zone, the military commander of the occupying power exercised absolute authority.

For issues common to Germany as a whole, the powers set up the Allied Control Council. In Berlin, the military commanders of each sector governed the city through the Kommandatura. In both the Allied Control Council and the Kommandatura, decisions required unanimous approval.

Only the Soviet Red Army entered Berlin by right of conquest, and between May and July 1945, it held exclusive control of the city. In Eastern Europe, the course of battle put American forces in areas that the allies had assigned to the Soviet Union. To emphasize their willingness to abide by the agreements, American policymakers withdrew troops back to their assigned zone of occupation in south-central Germany. They hoped this action would

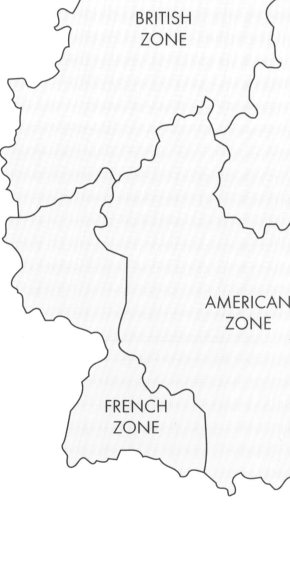

BRITISH ZONE

AMERICAN ZONE

FRENCH ZONE

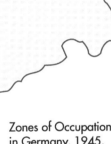

SOVIET
ZONE

● Berlin

Zones of Occupation
in Germany, 1945,
with Berlin in the
Soviet zone

Symbolizing the wartime alliance,
a U.S. Army infantryman greets a
Russian soldier in front of a sign
marking the historic meeting of the
Russian and American armies at
the Elbe, April 25, 1945.

1200

1300

1400

1500

1600

1700

1800

1900

1910

1920

1930

1940
1941
1942
1943
1944
1945

induce the Soviet Union to allow allied access to Berlin. In addition, the United States hoped to gain Soviet support and participation in the Pacific war against Japan and to preserve the existing alliance in Europe into the postwar period.

Occupied City

As American combat forces withdrew from Eastern Europe, the Soviets allowed American and British troops into Berlin. American and British forces thus arrived in Berlin in July 1945 by diplomatic compromise, not from the disposition of battle.

At British insistence, the French received a small zone of occupation in western Germany and a small sector in Berlin. The British prime minister wanted France involved in Germany because of the expressed American intention to withdraw all troops within two years. France represented a potential counterbalance to Soviet might and influence. The Soviet Union approved the inclusion of France so long as the territory accorded France came from the areas assigned to the other two powers and not from its assigned territories.

By supplanting the German institutions of state with the four-power regime of occupation and by dividing German territory among themselves, the allies hoped to exorcise German power from the community of nations. By dividing Berlin, they sought to deprive the German people of the historic focal point of their former national unity and glory. For the next 45 years, Berlin's destiny remained in the hands of the powers that occupied the city in mid-1945.

"I remember when word was spread that the West Allies would come to Berlin, in June or July of 1945, I was twelve. I [was] in the British sector. I was running around trying to meet some Brits in order to try my English."

Klaus Bartels, Berliner

FRENCH SECTOR

BRITISH SECTOR

AMERICAN SECTOR

SOVIET
SECTOR

Much of Berlin's historic architecture, including the Alte Museum in the Soviet sector, was severely damaged during World War II, and streets were littered with the machinery of war.

American Occupation in Berlin
1945–1948

Once the statesmen of the four allied powers had reached a political agreement, American troops withdrew from Eastern Europe and moved to Berlin. Advance parties from the American Army arrived in Berlin in late June. The destruction that they found in the city shocked even battle-hardened soldiers.

American Forces Arrive in Berlin

By arrangement with the Soviet army, American military forces began to arrive in Berlin during the first days of July 1945. On July 4, American troops assembled in the parade grounds of the former Prussian Military Cadet Academy (Hauptkadetten-anstalt) to assume formal control of the American sector. The ceremony included representatives of all four military contingents in the city: the British and the French as well as the Americans and the Soviets. While awaiting the acquisition of more permanent quarters, American troops set up tents in the Grünewald, the 11,000-acre public park along the western border of the American sector.

General Dwight D. Eisenhower, who commanded all American forces in the European theater, had visited Berlin in early June for the first meeting of the

"The bomb damage in the heart of the city is hard to describe. In certain areas the stench of unburied dead is almost overpowering. From Tempelhof to the Wilhelmstrasse not one undamaged building is standing; roofs, floors, and windows are gone; and in many cases the fragments of only one or two walls are standing. Many of the streets remain passable, but rubble covers the sidewalks, and large numbers of streets are still blocked off because of bomb craters and debris."

Colonel H. G. Sheen, U.S. Army advance team, reporting from Berlin, June 27, 1945

The Kaiser Wilhelm Memorial Church (Gedächtniskirche), a prominent landmark, was heavily damaged by bombs during the war.

Brandenburg Gate in 1945

four-power Allied Control Council. At that meeting, the four military commanders of the allied armies issued the Declaration of the Defeat of Germany and a proclamation announcing their assumption of supreme sovereign authority over the entire country. The proclamation asserted the authority of the Allied Control Council, in which the four powers acting together governed all of Germany. Eisenhower returned to Berlin late in July for the diplomatic conference at Potsdam, a Berlin suburb.

Lieutenant General Lucius D. Clay, Eisenhower's deputy commander in the theater and deputy military governor of the American occupation zone in Germany, represented American military interests in Berlin on a continuing basis. Clay was the commanding general of the American delegation on the Allied Control Council.

Clay's dual role as a deputy field commander and as the deputy military governor indicates the overlapping authorities exercised by the American military during the occupation. Especially in the weeks immediately after Germany's surrender, military commanders discharged both field command and command over civil government. American authorities established the Office of Military Government for Germany, United States (OMGUS) in October 1945 to control civic administration in the American zone. The lines of authority between civil and military command, although clear on paper, remained intertwined throughout the occupation.

American military officials examine damage to the German Parliament Building (Reichstag) in July 1945.

American forces arrived in Berlin in July 1945. Gen. Dwight D. Eisenhower, Commander, U.S. Forces, Europe, was welcomed by his deputy, Lt. Gen. Lucius D. Clay, deputy military governor of Germany.

American soldiers helped clear rubble in Berlin.

Damaged entrance to Reich Chancellery in Berlin, July 1945

The American military command in Berlin had the immediate mission of preparing for the visit by President Harry S Truman to the Potsdam Conference with British and Soviet leaders. In the weeks between the arrival of troops and the opening of the conference on July 17, soldiers had to open pathways through the streets and establish a communications system adequate to serve the president and his entourage.

Army engineers began work immediately in July 1945 to clear rubble from the streets to make them passable for normal traffic and for control of the population. Under the direction of the American soldiers, crews of Berliners that included a high proportion of women cleared the debris. They deposited the rubble around the city in mounds that grew into artificial hills as the collection of rubble continued over the next several decades. Landscaped, these hills provided land for general use. One of them, the Teufelsberg (Devil's Mountain) in the Grünewald, became the highest elevation in Berlin (120 meters) and later the site of British and American military installations.

As it prepared for the Potsdam Conference, the military command in Berlin had the long-term responsibility of establishing an effective governing authority in the American sector. This involved restoring the utilities and services basic to urban life, such as the water, sewer, electrical, and transportation systems. U.S. Army engineers rebuilt the city's street lighting system, returning over 1,000 natural gas street lamps to operation nine months after the arrival of Americans in Berlin. In their sector, American

British Prime Minister Clement Attlee, U.S. President Harry Truman, and Soviet leader Josef Stalin met at the Potsdam Conference, held between July 17 and August 2, 1945.

FRENCH SECTOR

BRITISH SECTOR

AMERICAN SECTOR

With public utilities out of order, German civilians pumped water out of sewers. The sign, one of hundreds placed in the city by the Russian Army, asserts the Red Army's rejection of racial hatred, "even against the German people," and its commitment to equal rights for all races and peoples.

The American sector of Berlin covered 81 square miles in the southwest quadrant of the city.

SOVIET
SECTOR

"Die Stärke der Roten Armee besteht darin, daß sie keinen Rassenhass gegen andere Völker, auch nicht gegen das deutsche Volk hegt und hegen kann, daß sie im Geiste der Gleichberechtigung aller Völker und Rassen, im Geiste der Achtung der Rechte anderer Völker erzogen ist."
/Stalin/

troops restored to operation 96 percent of the primary rail lines by February 1946.

The war had disrupted normal patterns of employment. In the American sector, 70,000 people out of the sector's total population of 500,000 had no jobs. The Army operated 72 different vocational training and placement programs for the sector's inhabitants. The Army itself employed substantial numbers of Berliners. For these workers, the monetary wage they received had far less value than the one hot meal a day that the Army provided for them. In postwar Berlin, this meal gave some workers the day's only nourishment.

To billet the occupation troops and to accommodate its administrative staff, the American command took control of facilities still fit for use. The American military confiscated properties that had belonged to the Nazi Party or to high party officials. For its headquarters, the American command confiscated nearly a dozen badly damaged structures of the former German East Air Defense Command Headquarters on Kronprinzenallee.

In July 1945, American forces also took over Berlin's main airport, Tempelhof, located in the American sector near the heart of Berlin. The arc-shaped terminal, designed to resemble an eagle in flight, had been planned in the early 1930s at the direction of Adolf Hitler, and 80 percent of the facility had been completed when construction was suspended in 1943. Bombing and systematic destruction by the invading

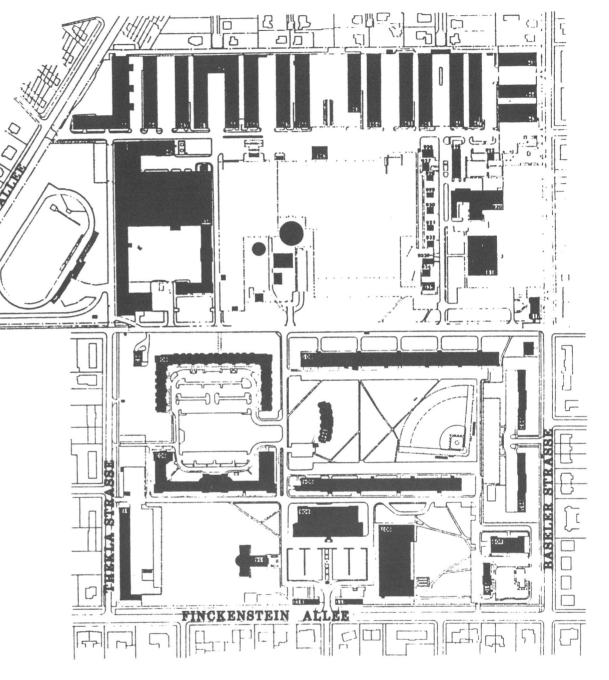

The 109-acre site of the Prussian Cadet Academy had been used during the Nazi years by Hitler's personal bodyguard (the Leibstandarte Adolf Hitler). Confiscated in July 1945, it was renamed Andrews Barracks in honor of wartime casualty Lt. Gen. Frank M. Andrews.

The U.S. Army established headquarters on Kronprinzenallee in facilities formerly used by the German air force.

The arc-shaped terminal of Tempelhof air base is a mile from end to end.

Russian forces had left both the terminal and the landing strip nearly useless.

With Tempelhof in American hands, troops began reconstruction by clearing away debris and restoring utilities. The airfield had only a sod runway, so the 862nd Engineer Aviation Battalion built a new 6,000-foot runway. Over a base of crushed brick from the rubble of the city, engineers poured a 2-inch layer of concrete. The concrete was then topped with pierced steel planks. When the airfield opened for military use, planes took off from the sod strip and landed on the pierced steel plank runway.

The military authorities requisitioned properties that belonged to private owners, allowing for compensation in a future settlement. Luxury residences became quarters for officers. The Army also took over other facilities needed to house troops and to provide services for the military community in Berlin. These acquisitions included substantial pieces of land, such as the 109-acre site of the former Prussian Cadet Academy, renamed Andrews Barracks. It was here that American troops had first formally taken control of their sector on July 4, 1945. The Army also acquired the formerly private Stubenrauch Hospital, confiscated by the Soviets in May. After repairs, it opened in December 1945 as a 72-bed hospital capable of expanding to 350 beds in emergencies.

Between August and October 1945, Berlin had postal service restored throughout the city for postcards and unsealed letters. By the end of

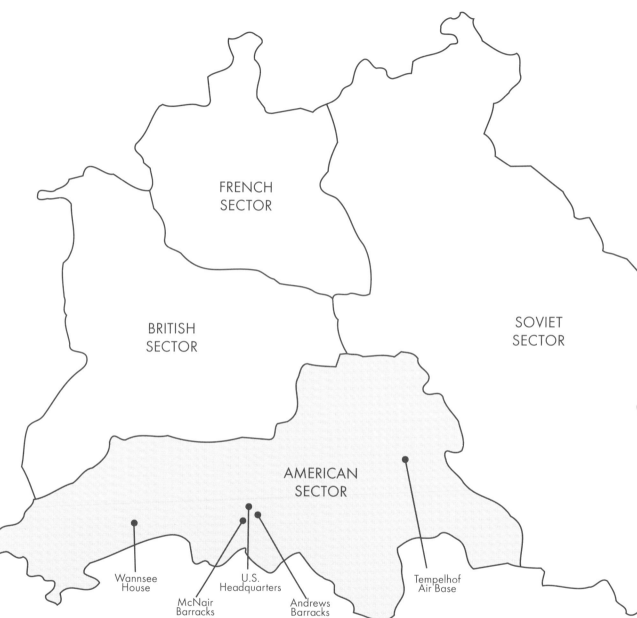

FRENCH SECTOR

BRITISH SECTOR

SOVIET SECTOR

AMERICAN SECTOR

Wannsee House

McNair Barracks

U.S. Headquarters

Andrews Barracks

Tempelhof Air Base

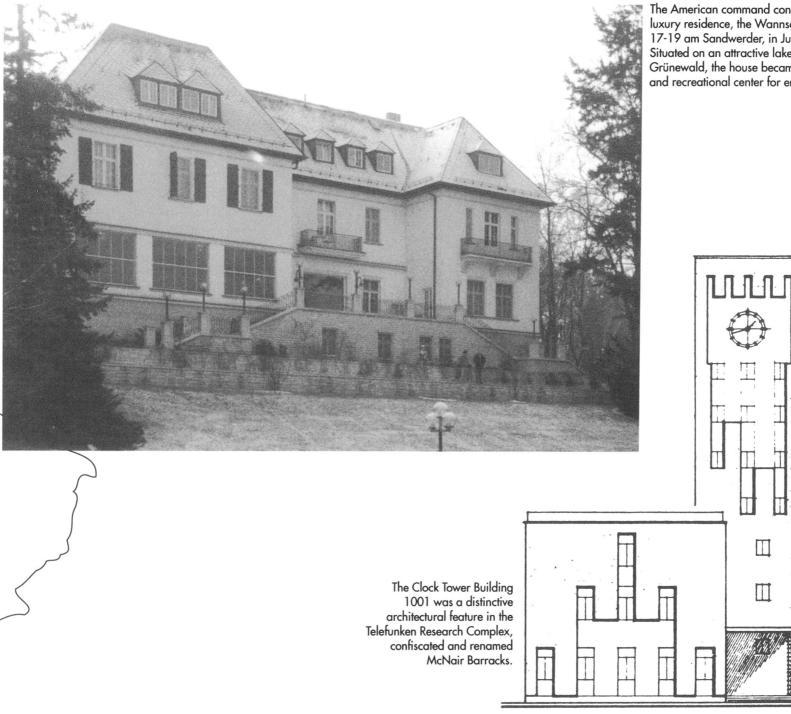

The American command confiscated a luxury residence, the Wannsee House at 17-19 am Sandwerder, in July 1945. Situated on an attractive lake in the Grünewald, the house became a hotel and recreational center for enlisted men.

The Clock Tower Building 1001 was a distinctive architectural feature in the Telefunken Research Complex, confiscated and renamed McNair Barracks.

1945
1946
1947
1948
1949
1950
1951
1952
1953
1954
1955
1956
1957
1958
1959
1960
1961
1962
1963
1964
1965
1966
1967
1968
1969
1970
1971
1972
1973
1974
1975
1976
1977
1978
1979
1980
1981
1982
1983
1984
1985
1986
1987
1988
1989
1990
1991
1992
1993
1994

October, mail service began throughout Germany among all four zones of occupation.

Organizing the American Sector

American troops arrived in Berlin trained to fight. As an occupying army they faced quite a different mission. American military forces in Germany also demobilized and redeployed so rapidly in the months after the German defeat that the command had to overcome the problems of rapid turnover and loss of personnel.

The Berlin Command addressed issues of personnel and training early in 1946. While the Army restructured troop formations in the American zone, the new Berlin Garrison reorganized troop units to form a lightly armed element called the Provisional Constabulary Squadron. Constabulary and military police units patrolled Berlin in cavalry scout cars to maintain order and to deal with the growing black market in rationed and controlled goods.

By the summer of 1946, American troop units in Berlin consisted of one battalion of infantry, one battalion of military police, the constabulary force, and a complement of service troops, about 6,700 soldiers in all. Although the units changed, that number remained relatively constant over the next 45 years.

The Berlin Command authorized military dependents to accompany service personnel beginning in April 1946. By the end of the year, about 100 military dependents lived in Berlin. Later, the number of dependents increased to several thousand, and so did the corresponding demand for facilities to support them: schools, family housing, commissaries, and post exchanges (PXs).

By the end of 1946, military authorities had reorganized command lines for the American occupation in Germany. The structure established in July 1945, U.S. Forces, European Theater (USFET), had evolved to include a headquarters and two subsidiary commands, one responsible for military operations and the other for military government in the American zone.

Between 1945 and March 1947, the commanding general of the American forces in Europe operated out of his headquarters in Frankfurt (the move to Heidelberg came in 1948). He oversaw both the military forces (USFET) and the Office of Military Government (OMGUS), which operated out of Berlin under General Clay. The commander in chief was most involved in military operations (as contrasted with the military government) throughout Germany and Austria. The distinction between military operations and military government was imprecise, especially since the main mission of the American military forces was to support the American military government in Germany.

The distinction became even more obscure in March 1947 when General Clay became commander in chief of the European Command (EUCOM), the successor to U.S. Forces, European Theater. As commander of the Office of Military Government, United States (OMGUS), Clay had been responsible since 1945 for issues concerning military government in the entire American zone, although he maintained OMGUS headquarters in Berlin, which was not in the American zone.

As a joint command, EUCOM incorporated the U.S. Air Forces in Europe (USAFE), and a small Navy contingent. Clay, now responsible for military operations, remained the commander of the military government. In Berlin and in Germany, he now commanded all American military forces, whether their primary task was in military government or in military operations.

"Housing was a unique situation there. It was all confiscated housing, so we had housing all over the city, along with large enclaves for the troops. But if you were a captain or higher, then you got out into the community, into some of the nicer areas. They were called villas and they had four-meter-high ceilings and chandeliers. . . . [Housing included] silverware. I mean silver silverware. Crystal—a complete set of crystal. Complete set of china—bone china."

Tom Starbuck, civilian employee, U.S. Army

Built in the 1920s and requisitioned by American forces in 1945, the house at 21 Finkenstrasse has been the residence of the commander, U.S. Army, Berlin, since 1954.

As the number of dependents in Berlin grew after 1946, so did the facilities to support them. This commissary in Andrews Barracks served from 1946 to 1949.

"After the war we requisitioned . . . some magnificent, old large German Bauhaus-type constructions. We gave many of them back after the war, but we kept about 115. Quite a few of the officers in Berlin are living in some of these old requisitioned properties."

Lieutenant Colonel Robert Baldinger, U.S. Army Corps of Engineers

1945
1946
1947
1948
1949
1950
1951
1952
1953
1954
1955
1956
1957
1958
1959
1960
1961
1962
1963
1964
1965
1966
1967
1968
1969
1970
1971
1972
1973
1974
1975
1976
1977
1978
1979
1980
1981
1982
1983
1984
1985
1986
1987
1988
1989
1990
1991
1992
1993
1994

Contacts with the Berliners

Initially, directives governing American military conduct in Berlin and Germany prohibited fraternization with the Germans. American soldiers seldom followed the policy, however, and it never took hold. By October 1945 the Army command had abandoned it.

Contacts between American soldiers and the children of Berlin developed rapidly. American GIs began informally to promote activities and games for Berlin's children, most of whom had precious little other than free time. These early encounters, which also occurred in the American zone in southern Germany, grew into a formal program that the Army adopted in the spring of 1946, the German Youth Activities Program. By tapping the exuberance of youth, American soldiers rapidly organized German Youth Activities clubs throughout the American sector of Berlin.

American military forces also established two radio stations in the early months of the occupation. Armed Forces Network (AFN) in Berlin began as an adjunct to the military command and was used to communicate informally with the troops. AFN first broadcast on August 4, 1945, from an improvised hut on the back of a truck, using a transmitter antenna strung between two trees. In succeeding months, AFN found studio space and increased its range of broadcasting. Over time it became one of the most listened-to radio stations in Berlin.

The only radio station in Berlin to survive the war, Radio Berlin, was in the Soviet sector, and

"I was fourteen or fifteen.... Most of [the clubs] were concentrated on sports like basketball and baseball, which was a new game....We had a swimming pool in the back. We had to clean this out ourselves. This is in Lichtenrade, way out south in the city in an old Nazi villa. There were eleven clubs. We had a theater group; we went to RIAS one day. Once a week the Americans came and they supplied us with records. And when we cleaned up, we got peanut butter and Coca-Cola. We had a dancing floor, we had ping-pong—table tennis. And all those things were completely new to us. We are a generation which grew up during the war, and we didn't have anything."

Helga Mellmann, Berliner

Formerly a German club, this building was used as the Quartermaster officers' club in 1945 and 1946. In 1947 it was converted into a German Youth Activities club, sponsored and maintained by the Quartermaster officers.

"I listened to AFN and heard all the be-bop, jazz, and then later on, of course, rock and roll.... These were the formative years.... They had these disc jockeys from AFN radio [who] were very popular.... Germans didn't know that style of announcing, this relaxed style and speaking to people. This was completely new."

Renate Semler, Berliner

Armed Forces Network broadcast, January 1951

1945
1946
1947
1948
1949
1950
1951
1952
1953
1954
1955
1956
1957
1958
1959
1960
1961
1962
1963
1964
1965
1966
1967
1968
1969
1970
1971
1972
1973
1974
1975
1976
1977
1978
1979
1980
1981
1982
1983
1984
1985
1986
1987
1988
1989
1990
1991
1992
1993
1994

the Soviets refused to allow western military authorities to use it. In November 1945, the American command therefore ordered the creation of a second radio station in the American sector to transmit to German civilians accurate information concerning occupation policies, hours of operation of the electric power system, the availability of rationed goods, possibilities of work, and other information pertinent to maintaining or restoring normal activities. The station, with the call letters RIAS (Radio in the American Sector), began broadcasting on February 7, 1946.

Because the American military had no wireless broadcasting equipment available in Berlin, RIAS's first programs traveled over the existing network of telephone wires in the American sector. Initial programming included the informational items that the command wanted, supplemented by news, music, light entertainment, and one daily broadcast in German. By September 1946, RIAS had begun wireless broadcasting, reaching most of the population of Berlin. Both AFN and RIAS developed into powerful elements of mass communication that Berliners turned to for information and entertainment.

In the months after Germany's defeat, the American military authorities established sufficient rapport with the population of Berlin to allow the governance of the American sector and the slow restoration of civic life. Controlling the German population proved in reality less difficult than achieving cooperation with the other three powers in governing Germany and Berlin.

Four-Power Occupation and Conflicts of Interest

The Cold War, that state of international tension between the United States and the Soviet Union that hovered just short of armed conflict, did not really begin over Germany. However, decisions by the two states concerning Germany sharpened the diplomatic contest because in Germany, particularly in Berlin, American and Soviet soldiers stood face to face.

The conferences of allied statesmen at Yalta (February 1945) and Potsdam (July 1945) had set democratization of Germany as one goal of the occupation, but democracy embodied different values for each of the powers. These differences became manifest through conflicts over a series of small issues. Who would supply food for the German population in each zone or sector? How much of German industrial capacity and stock of capital goods should be dismantled and removed? How restrictive would be the inter-zonal movement of people and goods? How would the four powers cooperate to administer and govern the four zones of occupation or the sectors of Berlin?

Each set of issues led to a clash of interests and intentions among the four occupying powers. Slowly, over the months between mid-1945 and mid-1948, disagreements sharply divided the western powers led by the United States on the one hand, from the Soviet Union on the other.

Members of the 7800th Infantry Platoon stand at attention, October 1947.

1945
1946
1947
1948
1949
1950
1951
1952
1953
1954
1955
1956
1957
1958
1959
1960
1961
1962
1963
1964
1965
1966
1967
1968
1969
1970
1971
1972
1973
1974
1975
1976
1977
1978
1979
1980
1981
1982
1983
1984
1985
1986
1987
1988
1989
1990
1991
1992
1993
1994

At stake was whose model of democracy, economy, and society would prevail in postwar Germany.

Berlin's Political Evolution

The Soviet Union had advantages in Berlin. Voters had strongly supported Marxist political parties in the years before Hitler's rise to power. In addition, the Soviets had exclusive control of the city from May to July 1945, before the agreements for the joint occupation of Berlin took effect.

The Red Army exercised a draconian occupation, however. The Soviets stripped the city, dismantling and removing over 380 factories from Berlin alone. They arrested and deported Berliners and refugees. The troops of the Red Army showed little discipline, engaging in pillage, rape, and often random murder. While some indiscipline and vengeance plagued all the occupying forces, the Red Army's conduct in Berlin was particularly harsh. Added to the traditional German antipathy toward the Russians, it strongly alienated Berliners.

During their exclusive tenure, the Soviet authorities freely appointed to municipal positions officials who were sympathetic to the Soviet Union and to communism. Their influence remained strong in the western sectors of Berlin even after authority was transferred to the other three occupying powers in July 1945. Berlin's geographic position—over 100 miles deep in the Soviet zone of occupation—put additional pressure on Berliners to get along with the Soviet Union.

Starting in July 1945 in eastern Germany and Berlin, the Soviet Union pushed to impose "democratic centralism," the Leninist political principle that concentrated power in the hands of a communist party elite to create a one-party dictatorship. The Soviet-appointed political leadership in eastern Germany promoted an anti-fascist front to unite all democratic parties against the return of Nazism. The Soviet-sponsored Communist Party of Germany (KPD) dominated the coalition. The Soviet Union advocated a similar united front throughout Germany and Berlin, hoping to co-opt the large following of the Marxist but democratically pluralistic German Social Democratic Party (SPD). In Eastern Europe, using similar tactics, the Soviets achieved total political control.

Their effort failed in Berlin. In March 1946 West German Social Democratic Party voters, responding in a plebiscite, resoundingly rejected fusion with the Communist Party. A few weeks

"I didn't lose my father in the war, but I lost my mother shortly after the war because she was shot by a Russian....This was September '45. It was in the Soviet zone. She was shot in the middle of the daylight. She was shot and died on the way to the hospital.... In my class there was always almost nobody who had two parents. It was mostly the father who was missing.... The usual type—father, mother—that was very rare."

Renate Semler, Berliner

In the midst of extensive damage to buildings on the Potsdamer Platz, Berliners began to pick up their lives again.

U.S. airmen arriving in Berlin in 1951 were surprised by the amount of rubble remaining in the city.

1945
1946
1947
1948
1949
1950
1951
1952
1953
1954
1955
1956
1957
1958
1959
1960
1961
1962
1963
1964
1965
1966
1967
1968
1969
1970
1971
1972
1973
1974
1975
1976
1977
1978
1979
1980
1981
1982
1983
1984
1985
1986
1987
1988
1989
1990
1991
1992
1993
1994

later, the Soviets forcibly merged the two parties in their zone and in eastern Berlin to form the Social Unity Party of Germany (SED). In municipal elections held in all four sectors in October 1946, the SED showed poorly, gaining less than 20 percent of the vote. The Social Democratic Party gained 48.8 percent, and two other parties founded on principles of democratic liberalism won an additional 33 percent.

The Social Democratic Party's share of the vote gave it control of the city council. It controlled appointment of the mayors in Berlin's municipal districts and elected its Berlin leader, Ernst Reuter, as mayor of the city. With Soviet support, however, the Social Unity Party forced the resignation of the Social Democratic Party's district mayors in the Soviet sector of Berlin and retained exclusive control there. In the four-power executive authority for Berlin, the Kommandatura, the Soviet commandant for Berlin vetoed Reuter's appointment as mayor.

Politics in Germany

In the portions of Germany controlled by the three western powers, the revitalization of German politics proceeded from the local to the regional level. In the American zone, occupation authorities permitted local elections beginning in January 1946. In February 1946, American authorities sponsored the first conference of minister presidents from the American and British zones. By June, the three states in the American zone had all elected assemblies to draw up their own constitutions and continued

to form state (Land) governments. French and British authorities promoted similar political activity. By the summer of 1947, all 11 German states in the three western zones had governments representing the electoral strength of democratically pluralistic parties. The German Communist Party fared very poorly in local and regional elections in the western zones.

In June 1947, leaders from all the German state governments met in Munich to discuss forming a new all-German state. Delegates from the five states that composed the Soviet zone in eastern Germany came to Munich, but left after one day when the other German leaders rejected their agenda for the discussions. The representatives of the states in the western zones continued the conference and, over the next two years, crafted the political documents to establish a German national government. Concurrently, relations between the western powers and the Soviet Union degenerated.

The Failure of Four-Power Cooperation

Politics evolved in Berlin and in Germany at the same time that Soviet and American interests openly diverged at the international level. The wartime agreements among the allies, confirmed at Potsdam in July 1945, provided that the four powers govern Germany as a single unit although they divided the country into zones of occupation for administrative purposes. These agreements broke down between 1945 and 1947.

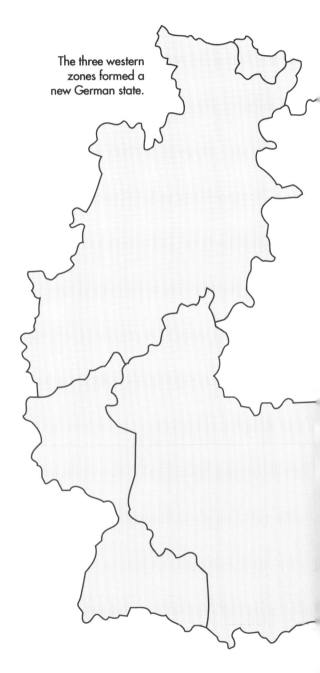

The three western zones formed a new German state.

Berlin

As deputy military governor of
Germany, Gen. Lucius Clay met
with the leaders of the three
German states (Länder) in the
American zone to discuss plans
for the new German government.

The Russians and the French both expected, and the other powers acknowledged, that Germany would pay reparations for devastating their homelands during the war. Difficulties arose over how much to extract. Both the Soviet Union and France expropriated industrial material and capital goods from their zones. As the expropriations continued, the German economy remained depressed below subsistence level. Great Britain had barely enough resources after the drain of the war to care for its own zone of occupation. Only the United States had the economic strength and the financial resources to reverse Germany's declining economy.

The American administrators in Germany faced an unenviable choice: to watch the German population in the west starve slowly; to import food, thereby shifting the cost of Soviet and French expropriation of German resources to the American taxpayers; or to try to stimulate the German economy so it could pay its own reparations and rebuild its resources. Policymakers in the United States chose the last option.

In May 1946, the American military governor, General Clay, suspended all deliveries of reparations outside the American zone, hoping to force all four powers to deal with the German economy as a whole. In July, American diplomats suggested that the three other allies merge the governments of all four zones to help the German economy recover. In September, American Secretary of State James F. Byrnes publicly renewed the offer in a major political address. He proposed to merge zones as part of a broad plan to give the German people more self-government. He spoke of Germany re-earning a place of honor among the free nations of the world.

The British responded positively to the plan to reorganize the occupation regime. On January 1, 1947, the British and the Americans merged the administration of their two zones to create Bizonia and began to formulate joint economic policies.

Currency Reform

Bizonia represented an effort to stimulate the German economy. Western planners became convinced that the economy needed a new currency that could inspire confidence and restore a flow of goods to market. Soviet planners resisted currency reform because such a plan assumed a capitalistic market economy that contradicted Soviet economic ideology. For similar reasons, the Soviet Union had earlier rejected participation in the Marshall Plan, proposed in June 1947 and launched throughout Western Europe in 1948.

The contest of wills between the Soviet Union and the United States over German economic recovery and currency reform became manifest in December 1947. That month the United States withdrew from the four-power London conference of foreign ministers when the Soviets rejected currency reform for Germany. When the Allied Control Council met in Berlin in March 1948, the four powers had made no progress toward compromise.

By normal rotation of the council presidency, the Soviet military commander chaired the meeting and used his presiding authority to adjourn the Allied Control Council with no date for a future meeting. The action effectively eliminated the one agency responsible under the diplomatic agreements to govern Germany as a whole. Four-power governance in Germany and Berlin had reached an impasse by the spring of 1948. Resolving the crisis divided Germany and Berlin between East and West.

"It started—Amerika Haus here in Berlin—as a moveable library in vans. The books were given by the military. GIs gave their books. . . . That could have been in '47, or so. As you know, all the books by contemporary American authors—not only Freud in the Jewish tradition, but also Americans—were banned. In the Nazi era, you didn't get these books."

Renate Semler, Program Director, Amerika Haus, Berlin

An exhibit on the Marshall Plan at Amerika Haus, Berlin, in June 1948 explained the European Recovery Program to strengthen economic development by promoting cooperation across national boundaries.

The Blockade of Berlin
and the Allied Airlift, 1948–1949

Tensions between the United States and the Soviet Union worsened after the Allied Control Council adjourned in March 1948. Following its suspension of meetings of the council, the Soviet Union closed highways and rail lines to Berlin through its zone beginning April 1, 1948.

Clay's Dilemma

The Soviet blockade of Berlin created an immediate problem. Supplies for the Berlin military community traveled from western Germany across the Soviet zone. West Berlin depended on the surrounding countryside of the Soviet zone for food and fuel and on overland traffic for its industrial supplies.

General Lucius Clay, who commanded American military forces and the American military government in Germany, recognized that the blockade threatened to force the city to accept Soviet authority or face strangulation. Clay did not want to withdraw American military forces from the city, thus conceding it to the Soviet Union. Instead, he proposed that the United States, with support from France and Great Britain, mount a combat force and send it across the Soviet zone to Berlin.

Such a challenge risked war. Secretary of State George C. Marshall consulted the Joint Chiefs of Staff concerning the readiness of American forces. They replied that the military would need at least 18 months to mobilize and prepare for war should the Soviets resist an armed column traversing their zone of occupation. President Truman decided that the risk precluded a direct military challenge to the Soviet Union.

To solve his immediate problem, supplies for his soldiers and their dependents, General Clay turned to air power. As a short-term measure, he mobilized all available aircraft to bring essential supplies to the military garrisons of the western powers in Berlin. The Soviets harassed the incoming flights, and one Soviet fighter plane even collided with a British military transport over Gatow airfield in the British sector, killing 12 British and 2 American servicemen.

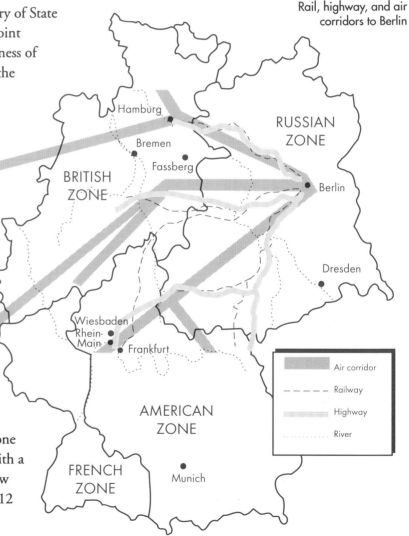

Rail, highway, and air corridors to Berlin

Hamburg

Bremen

Fassberg

BRITISH ZONE

RUSSIAN ZONE

Berlin

Dresden

Wiesbaden
Rhein-Main
Frankfurt

AMERICAN ZONE

FRENCH ZONE

Munich

Air corridor

Railway

Highway

River

Within a day, the Soviets lifted their restrictions on overland traffic, but their mini-blockade of Berlin warned of the crisis to come.

Clay saw clearly the challenge to the western powers in Berlin. In a telegram to his superiors in Washington, he argued:

> We've lost Czechoslovakia and we're in danger of losing [Finland]. If we intend to hold Europe against Communism, we dare not move from this position. I believe that the future of democracy demands that we stay put.

The crisis over how to deal with the German economy did not end once the Soviets had lifted their brief blockade of Berlin in early April 1948. The United States, France, and Great Britain maintained their resolve to implement financial reforms in Germany. In June, the three governments announced plans to introduce currency reform. In response, the Soviet commandant withdrew from the four-power executive agency for Berlin, the Kommandatura, on June 16, 1948.

The Blockade

The western allies introduced the new currency, the deutschmark, into their three zones of occupation, but not into their sectors of Berlin, on June 20. Three days later, the Soviets countered by circulating their own new currency in their zone and in Berlin. The Soviet commander in Germany declared all other currency, including the deutschmark, to be illegal throughout eastern Germany and in all of Berlin. That same evening, the Soviets cut electrical power to the western sectors of Berlin. Early on June 24, they closed road

and rail connections into Berlin. Over the next several days, they also stopped barge and water traffic. These measures effectively sealed Berlin off from all overland contact with the West, isolating it within the Soviet zone of occupation.

Currency reform served as the Soviet pretext for blockading Berlin. Soviet leaders quickly made their strategy clear. They would hold Berlin hostage until the allies halted the political developments in the western zones to create a West German government.

Beginning the Airlift

As in April, General Clay turned to the air. No one had ever tried to supply a city by using air transportation. Air power had worked on a small scale in April. The onus for aggressive action fell on the Soviet Union when the British plane crashed. If the Soviets took similar action again, they would face the same negative reaction in world opinion.

Moreover, the air corridors used by allied military air traffic had a status in international law that the land routes did not. The four powers had negotiated a document, signed by the Soviets in November 1945, that defined three corridors for American, French, and British use across the airspace of the Soviet zone to Berlin. No similar document, only constant practice, attested to the right of the western powers to use the autobahn, rail lines, or waterways to Berlin. Finally, the airlift bought time so the powers might explore a diplomatic resolution of the crisis.

"*If you landed on the left runway [at Tempelhof], you came down between the buildings over a graveyard, and if you landed on the right runway, you came over an eight-story building; and the end of the runway was right across the street . . . so it was over the building, chop off your power, push the yoke forward, pull it back, and you were on the ground. If you missed your approach, you did not go around but flew back to Frankfurt, landed, got in line, and flew to Berlin again.*"

Mark Taylor, U.S. Navy pilot in the airlift

"At Tempelhof the runways were about 5,000 feet and that was all. On either end of the runway you had buildings. . . . The planes would come in at a certain elevation, and after they cleared the building, they would have to go down and take a rather steep angle approach and then level out and get to use as much of the runway as they could.

"On the end of the runway, we took a dozer, and we dug an eight-foot-deep trench all the way across. . . . The purpose of that trench at the end was when they went over the end of the runway, [they would] lose their landing gear in the ditch. . . . We burned up two planes with the nose of the plane resting on the streetcar tracks in the middle of the street."

Major General Norman Delbridge, U.S. Army, retired

To launch the airlift, Clay ordered the United States Air Forces in Europe (USAFE), to make every aircraft in the European theater available to fly goods to Berlin. USAFE commanded about 100 C-47 transport planes, each capable of carrying about 3½ tons of cargo, but only two of the larger C-54s, each capable of carrying about 13 tons of cargo. Orders quickly went out to shift transport aircraft to Europe from other theaters: 11 planes left from Panama and 9 from Alaska on June 28; another 11 left from Hawaii the following day; others came from Massachusetts, Texas, Montana, the Caribbean, the Azores, and from as far away as Tokyo.

American crews flew the first missions of the airlift on June 26, the Saturday after the Soviets imposed the blockade. They carried 80 tons of milk, flour, medicine, and other cargo in 32 flights by C-47 aircraft. By the following Monday, the corridors carried a steady parade of airplanes into Berlin. The flights boosted morale in Berlin, but they did not answer the critical question: could the airlift supply a whole city of over 2 million people with all the goods needed to survive an indefinite blockade? Russian strategists did not think so. Even western planners had doubts.

The airlift began as a makeshift response to a sudden crisis. Early command decisions enhanced its likelihood of long-range success. The airlift's first commander set a goal of flying 65 percent of the available aircraft each day; the remainder underwent maintenance so

Tempelhof air base became the primary receiving point for airlift flights.

Sacks of flour on board a C-54

34

planes were always ready as replacements. Second, he ordered each aircraft to make three round trips to Berlin each day, reducing the ground time required to replace planes after each trip. Third, he dispatched aircraft in like batches. All the C-47s flew in succession, then all the C-54s. In this way, planes with the same cruising speed could maintain constant intervals and air traffic would move more smoothly. Finally, he centralized air traffic control at a facility in Frankfurt that scheduled all airlift flights.

These command decisions in the first days of operations led to initial successes. Airplanes flying from Rhein-Main and Wiesbaden air bases in the American zone to Tempelhof air base in West Berlin delivered 1,000 tons of goods in one 24-hour period on July 7, an important milestone. On July 30, American fliers set a record by delivering 1,918 tons in a single day. Almost daily thereafter the tonnage increased.

Barrels of machine oil were loaded at Rhein-Main for the flight to Berlin.

Milk loaded
on a C-47
at Rhein-Main

Planes arriving at Tempelhof were
loaded with supplies to sustain
both the military garrisons and
the citizens of West Berlin.

Maintaining the Airlift

Berliners and displaced persons in Berlin supplied the work crews necessary to service the airlift, often working alongside American troops. The Army curtailed its normal field training in the Grünewald to reassign personnel as guards and checkers at Tempelhof. Army engineer troops and officers organized construction crews to expand the capacity of the airfields to receive planes.

The constant operation of flights in and out of airfields put heavy demands on the limited landing facilities in Berlin. Tempelhof had only one surfaced runway when the airlift began, and it had been built for light aircraft, not for the constant pounding of repeated landings by transport planes. The base course on the runway began to sag almost immediately under the weight of heavily loaded C-47s and C-54s, and the concrete shell broke. Aided by teams of Berliners, U.S. Army engineers reinforced the sagging base course with crushed rubble gathered from the wartime ruins of Berlin and laid pierced steel plank over the runway.

Taking positions along the runway, work crews would rush onto the field between landings, lift the plank surface at the failing spots, fill the cavities with a mixture of sand and bitumen, bend back the planks to the correct position, and weld steel straps between them. Each work team had a lookout who warned of the next incoming aircraft. This procedure kept the runway in operation around the clock, but a single

Workers repaired the older runway at Tempelhof with pierced steel planking, sand, hot tar, and asphalt as planes flew overhead, August 1948.

runway could never handle the number of landings that the airlift needed to succeed

Constructing New Runways

The allies needed more landing space in Berlin if the airlift were to succeed. U.S. Army engineers received orders on July 8, 1948, to construct a second pierced steel plank runway at Tempelhof. They completed construction within 49 days of the initial survey and had the runway in operation by September 8. They also began a third runway, this one of asphalt, on August 23. Also in late August, American aircraft began using Gatow airfield in the British sector.

American aircraft at Gatow airfield

Building the new runway at Tempelhof started with Trümmerfrauen (rubble women) loading rubble onto a truck. Trucks and bulldozers then laid the rubble foundation.

Airlift flights continued while U.S. Army engineers constructed a new runway at Tempelhof beginning in August 1948.

1945
1946
1947
1948
1949
1950
1951
1952
1953
1954
1955
1956
1957
1958
1959
1960
1961
1962
1963
1964
1965
1966
1967
1968
1969
1970
1971
1972
1973
1974
1975
1976
1977
1978
1979
1980
1981
1982
1983
1984
1985
1986
1987
1988
1989
1990
1991
1992
1993
1994

42

To expand capacity even further, American Army engineers built an entirely new airfield at Tegel in the French zone in an area formerly used by the German military for maneuvers. Crews worked around the clock in three shifts, seven days a week. At the peak of construction, about 17,000 workers, nearly half of whom were women, labored at Tegel. Workers received 1.20 deutschmarks a day plus a hot meal.

Construction at Tegel began without the heavy equipment needed for efficient work—rollers, graders, bulldozers—because these pieces of equipment were too large to fit into the available aircraft. The engineers solved the problem by cutting them into sections for transport and then welding them back together in Berlin. Over time, the airlift transported approximately 40 pieces of heavy equipment for use on airfield construction. Just three months after they began construction at Tegel in August, Army engineers completed the airfield, which began receiving airlift flights on November 5, 1948.

Large pieces of equipment had to be cut apart, airlifted to Berlin, then welded back together. Army engineers completed the reassembly of this rock crusher on August 27, 1948.

"We had more women than men that did all the earth moving.... These people would work for one ladle of potato soup and a big chunk of black bread. And they moved the earth by hand. We had some equipment, but nothing that could move earth. The Germans have these little mine cars and they can lay these little tracks all over everything.... They'd lay these little tracks and they'd throw the bricks in these little cars and push the cars by hand."

Major General Norman Delbridge, U.S. Army, retired

Berliners helped move earth in construction of the new runway at Tegel.

Increasing the Tempo

As more planes arrived in the western zones and the airlift's capacity to carry goods increased, the Air Force sought even greater efficiencies in airlift operations. It therefore reassigned management of the airlift to its new Military Air Transport Service (MATS) in late July 1948. The MATS commander rationalized flight paths through the access corridors to increase the efficient flow of planes between western Germany and Berlin. Planners worked to coordinate each aspect of the airlift and to standardize every procedure so each flight, from loading to discharge and return, would proceed in exactly the same way.

The MATS commander set as his goal one flight for each of the 1,440 minutes of a 24-hour day. He wanted the airlift to operate with a rhythm as "constant as the jungle drums." The airlift never achieved the goal, but it approached it more closely than anyone imagined possible. It did achieve three-minute intervals as a nearly standard daily tempo, and crews made a one-day record-breaking run of 1,398 flights.

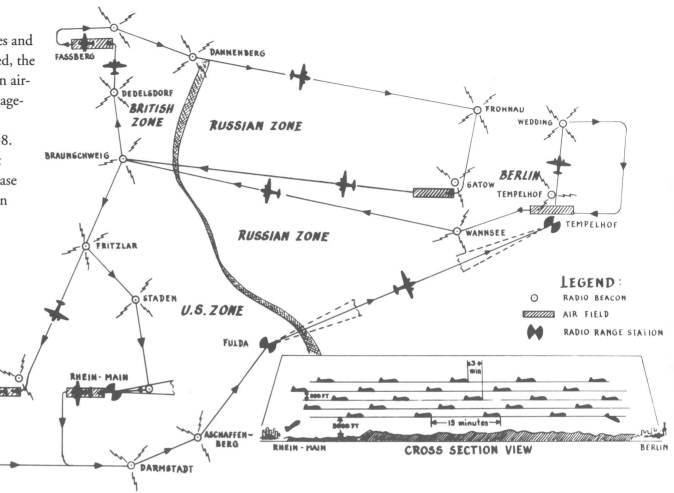

Air corridors and placement of Army Airways Communications System navigational aids for the Berlin airlift

AACS personnel improvised new methods of air traffic control to handle the volume of air traffic. Flight plans, position reports, and clearance phraseology were streamlined to limit the length of radio transmissions and accelerate operations. At the peak of the airlift, there were 90 AACS officers and 700 enlisted personnel serving.

During the airlift, planes left from three bases, Rhein-Main and Wiesbaden air bases near Frankfurt and the Royal Air Force base at Fassberg in the British zone. Aircraft from Wiesbaden and Rhein-Main flew to Berlin along the southern corridor and returned via the central corridor. Aircraft from Fassberg flew to Berlin along the northern corridor and returned via the central corridor. Radio beacons and ranges guided planes along the routes.

Traffic at Tempelhof was
heavy on the ground
and in the air.

"I was 27 years old, single, and a lieutenant (jg) in the United States Navy
when ordered to fly the Berlin airlift....
When you reported over [Berlin], you were
radar identified by the radar site that
would keep you in line and in the corridor,
which was 10 miles wide but seemed like
10 feet."

Mark Taylor, U.S. Navy pilot in the airlift

Coal, necessary for heating and for generating electricity, composed about 40 percent of the airlift tonnage. The airlift transported fuel oil, medical supplies, and other goods, besides food. Operations on the ground received the same meticulous attention that flight plans did, so loading and unloading went as efficiently as possible. The attention to procedures reduced unloading time from 17 to 5 minutes and re-fueling time from 33 to 8 minutes. Overall, the time to turn the aircraft around in Berlin dropped from an hour to 30 minutes.

Crews unloaded flour from rail cars and into trucks at Wiesbaden.

Bags of coal wait at Rhein-Main to be airlifted to Berlin.

"*At Tempelhof we pulled into line and DPs [displaced persons] unloaded our aircraft by picking up a 50-pound bag under each arm and dropping them on a slide that went to a truck. We used to give them cigarettes if they would hurry it up so we could get back in line for takeoff sooner. They unloaded 20,000 pounds manually in 8 to 10 minutes.*"

Mark Taylor,
U.S. Navy pilot in the airlift

Bags of flour
unloaded from
planes at
Tempelhof

1945
1946
1947
1948
1949
1950
1951
1952
1953
1954
1955
1956
1957
1958
1959
1960
1961
1962
1963
1964
1965
1966
1967
1968
1969
1970
1971
1972
1973
1974
1975
1976
1977
1978
1979
1980
1981
1982
1983
1984
1985
1986
1987
1988
1989
1990
1991
1992
1993
1994

Berliners and Americans

The long-term success of the airlift began to appear possible by late July 1948. Its ultimate success depended on the will of the West Berliners, however, because the Soviets controlled all the essential supplies within easy access of Berlin. To undermine the resolve of West Berliners, Soviet authorities offered food and heating fuel at sharply reduced prices. In return, they asked for an individual's pledge not to accept food and goods from the allied airlift. Only about 1 percent accepted the Soviet offer.

Although Berliners showed great determination to maintain their independence and good humor, they welcomed every gesture to improve morale. A young Air Force pilot, Lieutenant Gail S. Halvorsen, initiated his own effort that endeared him to a generation of Berliners. He attached candy to tiny make-shift parachutes and dropped it for children as he made his approaches over Tempelhof. Halvorsen began his initiative privately. It had such a positive reception in the city, however, that the airlift commander organized the drops and established collection points for candy and for handkerchiefs to make the small parachutes. He also set up special flights for Halvorsen and other pilots to pass over the entire city, dropping candy even in the Soviet sector.

In November 1948, Americans also aided more than 2,000 students and professors who left the University of Berlin, situated in the Soviet sector, because of the oppressive atmosphere. With support from American universities and from

In *Operation Little Vittles*, Capt. Eugene T. Williams dropped candy attached to miniature parachutes for the children of Berlin.

After the airlift, U.S. Air Force Lt. Gail S. Halvorsen, "The Candy Bomber," met with some of the Berlin children who received the candy he dropped.

"It was so terrible. CARE packete [packages] was a word but we never saw one. I dreamed of CARE packete. I don't know how they [other Berliners] managed to get them.

"During that winter, we were living in the kitchen. Most times there was no electricity. We still had an oven combination with gas and fireplace. The fire was not just to give you warmth, but to give you light. . . . And what we got to feed the oven was not briquettes, it was the dust, coal dust. . . . When you read that there was enough food provided, that's definitely not correct."

Klaus Bartels, Berliner

"I used to put [extra clothes] on to go to bed, because I was so cold. We had one room which we could heat. My mother woke up in the middle of the night to do the cooking."

Helga Mellmann, Berliner

1945
1946
1947
1948
1949
1950
1951
1952
1953
1954
1955
1956
1957
1958
1959
1960
1961
1962
1963
1964
1965
1966
1967
1968
1969
1970
1971
1972
1973
1974
1975
1976
1977
1978
1979
1980
1981
1982
1983
1984
1985
1986
1987
1988
1989
1990
1991
1992
1993
1994

the Ford Foundation, the dissenting students and faculty founded a new institution in the American sector, the Free University of Berlin.

Christmas 1948 approached, and no break appeared in the impasse between the Soviet Union and the western powers. American military personnel gathered presents for Berlin's children. Hollywood entertainer Bob Hope brought his comedy and musical review to Berlin to cheer American soldiers and airmen.

The Costs of the Airlift

West Berliners paid a price to maintain their freedom. Privation was real and serious for the population of Berlin for whom food and fuel remained scarce. Unemployment rose steadily because industries did not have sufficient fuel to operate.

American and British taxpayers bore a different burden in the Berlin airlift. Shipping each ton of supplies flown to Berlin cost about $100, and the airlift as a whole cost an estimated $200 million.

The Berlin airlift cost more dearly than money. Although it was remarkably safe—in 276,926 flights only 17 American and 7 British planes crashed—still 76 persons died in airlift operations, including 31 American servicemen. Berliners did not forget those who gave their lives.

On July 25, 1948, a C-47
Skytrain crashed into this
building, killing both pilots.

The Success of the Airlift

Severe weather during the winter of 1948–49
did not stop the airlift from delivering cargo to
Berlin. The winter's heaviest snow fell on March 1,
1949, but it hardly affected the tempo of deliveries. To demonstrate its capacity to supply
Berlin indefinitely, the Military Air Transport
Service staged a one-day push for Easter
Sunday, April 16, 1949. This
"Easter Parade" achieved the
record 1,398 flights, nearly
one flight a minute for 24
hours, and delivered 12,941
tons of goods to Berlin.

Airlift flights continued around
the clock and through the heavy
snowfall of March 1, 1949.

By the spring of 1949, the Soviets recognized that their siege of Berlin had failed. They could neither cut off nor bribe the population of West Berlin. Nor could they disrupt the political process in the western zones by threatening Berlin. In early May, the Parliamentary Council, representing the German voters in the three western zones, completed a draft document to create a West German state. The document won an overwhelming vote of approval on May 4. On May 12, the Soviets lifted the blockade of Berlin.

General Clay remained suspicious that the Soviet Union might reimpose the blockade once the allies had dismantled the organization that sustained the airlift. He therefore ordered the continuation of the airlift to build up stockpiles of goods in the city. The practice of maintaining stockpiles of essential goods continued in West Berlin into following decades. The final airlift flight took place on September 30, 1949.

By the time the airlift ended, Europe had a new structure for mutual defense in the North Atlantic Treaty Organization (NATO). Sixteen nations led by the United States pledged themselves to defend the boundaries of Western European states, including western Germany. The three western zones of Germany had formed a new government, the Federal Republic of Germany (FRG), and the Soviet Union had created the German Democratic Republic (GDR) in its zone. The Cold War division of Europe between East and West had hardened.

U.S. Navy flight and ground crews in squadron VR-6 celebrated the end of the blockade.

To build reserves in Berlin, the allies continued the airlift until September 30, 1949.

"The more I got involved in this [story of the airlift], the more I realized that the whole thing—it's not American Air Force history, not American history, it's world history. If the Berliners would not have stood to their word, all of Europe would be under the Communist regime."

Helga Mellmann, photographer with the U.S. Air Force in Berlin, 1962–1993

The last plane to Berlin in the airlift carried a load of coal and a group of press correspondents.

The American Bond with Berlin
1949–1958

As West Germany's economy recovered in the 1950s, differences between the politics, the economies, and the ideologies of West and East became starkly evident in Berlin. West Berlin shared in the growing prosperity, and its citizens enjoyed economic opportunities and a freedom of expression not found in East Berlin. For those living within Soviet-controlled East Germany, West Berlin functioned as a showcase for the political and economic advantages in the western system.

Cold War Realignment

The success of the airlift reinforced the rearrangement of political forces in European and world affairs that had developed slowly after World War II. For the states of Western Europe, the development led to an alliance, led by the United States, in a voluntary coalition of nations pledged to defend each other's territorial integrity. Mutual interest and mutual consent bound the allies who formed the North Atlantic Treaty Organization in 1949.

By contrast, the postwar conduct of the Soviet Union in Eastern Europe and Berlin convinced Western European leaders that coercion characterized the Soviet system of alliances.

Western governments and most of their people found the Soviet Union hostile to free and open political and economic development.

Events outside Europe aggravated western anxiety and the mistrust of Soviet intentions. In September 1949, President Truman announced that the Soviet Union had exploded an atomic bomb, ending the American monopoly of nuclear weapons. Within weeks of that shock, the long civil war in China ended in victory for the Chinese Communist Party. The party's leader, Mao Zedong, took power in the new People's Republic of China on October 1, 1949.

The conduct of North Korea, the Soviet Union's client state, provoked even greater alarm. After the end of the Pacific war, the United States had kept American troops in the south of the Korean peninsula, partitioned like Germany between two

A small, pocket-size brochure, issued by the commander in chief, U.S. Army, Europe, Gen. Thomas T. Handy, explains the importance of the soldier's mission in Germany, admonishing him to be "fair and honorable in dealings with the German people," and to be an "effective ambassador of good will" for America at all times.

1945
1946
1947
1948
1949
1950
1951
1952
1953
1954
1955
1956
1957
1958
1959
1960
1961
1962
1963
1964
1965
1966
1967
1968
1969
1970
1971
1972
1973
1974
1975
1976
1977
1978
1979
1980
1981
1982
1983
1984
1985
1986
1987
1988
1989
1990
1991
1992
1993
1994

governments. In late June 1950, the North Koreans launched a full-scale military attack on South Korea. The momentum of the attack threatened to overrun both South Korean and American forces. American and European leaders feared that the attack on South Korea presaged a similarly aggressive approach in Central Europe and divided Germany.

In Germany itself, political evolution reinforced the division of the country. The process that led to the Federal Republic of Germany in 1949 also placed this newborn state squarely on the western side in an increasingly divided Europe. In its zone, the Soviet Union sponsored the German Democratic Republic, a thinly veiled one-party dictatorship.

Rearranging Authority

As the Federal Republic of Germany held elections and formed a government, the western allies adjusted their responsibilities in Germany. Three civilian high commissioners, organized in the High Commission for Germany (HICOG), replaced the American, British, and French military governors in September 1949. The commissioners acted more as ambassadors than as occupying authorities, although the High Commission retained certain controls, including authority over West German constitutional provisions, internal legislation, and foreign policy decisions. The three western governments intended to retain these residual rights, which derived from their victory, only during the transition from occupation to self-government.

> "*I arrived in Berlin in September of 1951 and was there for three years.... I was kind of apprehensive about being 110 miles behind Russian troops. Coming in on the train was kind of spooky in itself. Everything was blacked out. You got on a train and they gave you a compartment and a pass saying, 'Don't look out the windows of the train or anything.' ... When we came out of Frankfurt and got into the East, we changed engineers to a German under Russian leadership.... Then [we changed again] when we got to Berlin.*"
>
> *Private James Bourk,*
> *U.S. Air Force, 1951–1954*

Travel orders in English and Russian (1951) for PFC James Bourk

This Christmas card from the early 1950s depicts the increasing tension and growing contrasts between East and West Berlin: prosperity versus scarcity, smiles versus frowns, and automobiles versus bicycles, with Clayallee in the West and Stalinallee in the East. The phrase "Ami Go Home" on the large street sign is addressed to American troops, derisively called "Ami."

Berlin was not officially a part of either the West German or the East German state. The West Germans who drafted the constitutional documents had incorporated Berlin as a city-state of the Federal Republic of Germany, but the western high commissioners objected. To include Berlin in the Federal Republic might compromise the four-power accords on which France, Great Britain, and the United States based their claim to maintain a military presence in the city. If West Germany could claim Berlin, why couldn't East Germany?

The western powers did not want to endorse a precedent that would give what the success of the airlift had denied to the Soviet Union: control of the entire city of Berlin. Representing the occupying powers with residual rights, the three western high commissioners vetoed the inclusion of Berlin in the Federal Republic.

The change from military government to civilian commissioners coincided with the reorganization of the American command. Major General Maxwell D. Taylor arrived in Berlin as the new senior commander in August 1949. When the Office of Military Government lapsed, Taylor's remaining responsibilities for military government and his military functions as U.S. commandant combined under a new title: U.S. Commander, Berlin (USCOB). He exercised authority over Army, Air Force, and Navy units in Berlin and continued to discharge both military and diplomatic functions. For military matters, he reported to the commander of U.S. Army, Europe, in Heidelberg. For diplomatic responsibilities, he reported to the senior

During the Cold War of the 1950s, the U.S. Army used posters to remind soldiers that they were stationed in Berlin to keep West Berlin free.

Maj. Gen. Maxwell Taylor, U.S. Commander, Berlin, visited an integrated Army education class at McNair Barracks, November 1949.

Three U.S. airmen assigned to the 7350th Base Complement Squadron at Tempelhof stand under the distinctive curved overhang of the air terminal.

1945
1946
1947
1948
1949
1950
1951
1952
1953
1954
1955
1956
1957
1958
1959
1960
1961
1962
1963
1964
1965
1966
1967
1968
1969
1970
1971
1972
1973
1974
1975
1976
1977
1978
1979
1980
1981
1982
1983
1984
1985
1986
1987
1988
1989
1990
1991
1992
1993
1994

State Department representative in Bonn, the capital of the Federal Republic of Germany.

Defending Berlin

Shortly after Taylor arrived, West Berlin faced a menacing campaign. In January 1950, East German leaders announced a forthcoming rally of the Free German Youth, a movement sponsored by the regime. Official propaganda spoke of a march in which patriotic young East Germans would force the West Berlin city government, alleged to be illegal and illegitimate, out of office.

In response, the American military command stepped up readiness drills. Soldiers increased bayonet practice and received special training in crowd and riot control. The French and the British coordinated similar activities with the American command. The exercises sent the message that the western powers would resolutely meet any violent action. The training also served to back up the preparations of the West Berlin police forces.

On the Sunday before the rally in East Berlin, the American command scheduled an open house at Tempelhof air base. Tens of thousands of Berliners toured the base and viewed the military equipment on display. A week later, the Free German Youth marched eastward from the Brandenburg Gate down the main avenue, Unter den Linden, rather than into West Berlin as threatened. The weekend passed with only minor incidents, but West Berliners recognized

that at any moment the East Germans could provoke a crisis.

Within weeks of the Free German Youth rally in East Berlin, war broke out in Korea, heightening anxiety over the possibility of similar Soviet action in Germany. The Korean conflict spurred the rapid buildup of a NATO military force, and the United States rushed more troops into France and West Germany. Between 1950 and 1952, American troop strength in Europe rose from fewer than 100,000 soldiers to more than 250,000.

In Berlin, the American military command retrained the constabulary squadron as infantry units, merged them into the reactivated 6th Infantry Regiment, and reorganized the military police units for combat readiness.

Simultaneously, the command began constructing facilities to support its soldiers, their equipment, and their families. By expanding and modernizing these installations, the command emphasized the American commitment to stay in Berlin. West Berlin's city government bore all the expenses of military construction as a part of the costs of the occupation.

In the early 1950s, the U.S. Army began constructing new stairwell apartment buildings to house the growing number of soldiers with families. Built with German deutschmarks by German contractors, these apartments combined American requirements with German design.

Houses such as the duplex at 414A Goldfinkweg were constructed in 1956 with German deutschmarks to house American military families.

U.S. Army Commander, Berlin Brigade, Brig. Gen. Charles S. D'Orsa presents keys for a new apartment in Andrews Barracks to the first occupants in November 1958. The building on Basslerstrasse provided apartments for 18 families and was one of two such units completed that year.

Soviet pressure on the city continued even after the Free German Youth rally. During the blockade, the eight municipal districts in East Berlin had withdrawn from city government under Soviet coercion. To adjust to the secession, the remaining districts of West Berlin drew up a new municipal constitution in 1950. The East Germans responded by briefly cutting off electric power to the western sectors of the city, just as they had at the beginning of the blockade in 1948. Similarly, the Soviets stopped barge traffic into West Berlin. Despite the pressure, the revised constitution was drafted and approved. It went into effect on October 1, 1950.

A new commissary
opened early in 1958.

Officials cut the ribbon for the Berlin-American School, which opened September 3, 1958, with 740 students in kindergarten through 12th grade.

The Outpost Theater, located on Clayallee near Truman Plaza, brought American movies to the soldiers and their families.

Such incidents of harassment continued episodically throughout the 1950s. In 1952 and 1953, Soviet fighter planes interfered with commercial and military aircraft in the corridors leading to Berlin. An Air France commercial carrier came under Soviet fighter attack in mid-1952. A Soviet aircraft buzzed an American hospital plane in October. Early in 1953, the Soviets shot down a British bomber flying a routine training mission. In response to each incident, the western allies issued diplomatic protests.

The military commands maintained troop readiness. French, British, and American soldiers began coordinated exercises in the Grünewald that developed into a joint bivouac for three days each autumn. American troops trained in Berlin and at other training areas in West Germany, particularly at Grafenwöhr.

"We got a call for an emergency out on the runway—a Pan American aircraft had come in. A gentleman had been shot. It was kind of funny, when we were opening up his trousers to see how bad he was shot, he had a wooden leg—a prosthesis. He wasn't injured that badly. But it sure makes you wonder and think about what can happen and what could happen from that kind of an incident.... [The Russians] claimed that this aircraft had flown out of the corridor, and, of course, they said they didn't."

Private James Bourk, U.S. Air Force, 1951–1954

Two Russian MIG-15 fighter jets attacked an Air France C-54 Skymaster as it approached Berlin in a routine commercial flight on the morning of April 5, 1952. The plane carried 11 passengers and a 5-person crew. The attack wounded 2 passengers, but the plane landed safely.

Roosevelt Barracks, built in 1884 and formerly the Prussian Ordnance Training School, became the home of the 6941st Guard Battalion (Labor Service) in 1950.

"By the end of August of 1950, the 6941st Labor Service Area was instituted. Later on, it was redesignated the 6941st Guard Battalion (Labor Service).... We were trained in fighting civil disturbance. The major function always was securing all U.S. installations.... Basically, the credo of the U.S. Command, Berlin, was: soldiers will not pull guard duty. They have other things to do. That's what the guard battalion is there for."

Klaus Bartels, retired commander of the 6941st

1945
1946
1947
1948
1949
1950
1951
1952
1953
1954
1955
1956
1957
1958
1959
1960
1961
1962
1963
1964
1965
1966
1967
1968
1969
1970
1971
1972
1973
1974
1975
1976
1977
1978
1979
1980
1981
1982
1983
1984
1985
1986
1987
1988
1989
1990
1991
1992
1993
1994

Economic Recovery

To encourage economic recovery in Germany, the western allies had implemented the currency reform that had triggered the Soviet blockade of Berlin. To further the economic recovery, the participants in the American-sponsored Marshall Plan agreed in late 1949 to include West Germany in its benefits. Because the blockade had brought dire economic conditions to Berlin, including 40 percent unemployment, the United States encouraged the Federal Republic of Germany to share its Marshall Plan funds with West Berlin.

The West Germans funneled over 1.2 million deutschmarks of the local funds generated from Marshall Plan activities (called counterpart funds) to West Berlin. There they helped create 150,000 new jobs and reduce unemployment to 20 percent of the labor force by late 1953. To expand the capacity of West Berlin's electrical generating plants and to lessen dependence on East German power, the United States made an additional 77 million deutschmarks available directly to the city.

An exhibit on display in July 1951 near the Kaiser Wilhelm Memorial Church showed Berliners the economic progress stimulated by the European Recovery Program (ERP), better known as the Marshall Plan.

"When we would have our leave, we could go anyplace. We could even go in the Russian sector. . . . In fact, when we would go over to the British sector or the French sector, especially the French sector, from Tempelhof, we would a lot of times get a cab. The cabbie would go right through the Russian sector. As long as you didn't cause any trouble or do anything wrong, they never bothered you."

Private James Bourk,
U.S. Air Force, 1951–1954

"When we'd go out and take a little stroll, we'd see pictures of the Marshall Plan [projects]. They were trying to rehabilitate the city and rebuild. And, as in a lot of the pictures you see, much of it was still bombed out. I'd say the majority [was still bomb-damaged], especially in the other sectors where they didn't have the Marshall Plan working as well as we did [in the American sector]."

Private James Bourk,
U.S. Air Force, 1951–1954

The East German Uprising of June 1953

American economic assistance encouraged West Berliners to invest their own time and effort in the recovery. East Berliners and East Germans received no comparable encouragement from the Soviet Union. Then in March 1953, Soviet dictator Josef Stalin, who had dominated the Russian and Soviet state since the early 1920s, died.

In the aftermath of Stalin's death, uncertainties about leadership in the Soviet Union raised expectations of change in East Germany, where much needed to be changed. Food shortages, a lack of raw materials, defective central planning, and continuing reparations to the Soviet Union burdened the people and the economy.

In late May 1953, the East German government announced increases in food prices and additional production quotas for workers that amounted to a cut in wages of over 40 percent. The measures provoked widespread protests, and in the following two weeks, workers staged intermittent work stoppages. On June 12, 13, and 15, workers in East Berlin received the first pay envelopes calculated on the new increased norms. They took to the streets in protest. On the morning of June 17, tens of thousands of workers from the railroads, steel mills, and textile factories began to march into the government district. A crowd massed outside an East German government building. Demonstrators climbed the Brandenburg Gate and tore down the red flag that flew atop it. In over 200 communities across East Germany, workers carried on similar demonstrations.

In the afternoon, the Soviet military command declared martial law in East Berlin and moved tanks and infantry into the city's center. As the East German police tried to disperse the crowds, riots broke out. Soviet tanks and troops moved in, sealed the sector border with West Berlin, and by nightfall had put down the riots. The East German regime blamed western agents for inciting the riots, held summary trials, meted out prison sentences, and executed several hundred demonstrators. In truth, the uprisings had their origins in the dismal economic situation and in the general unpopularity of the government.

Integration with the West

While the Soviet Union kept its client government in power by suppressing the spontaneous uprising of East German workers, the western allies negotiated to extend increasing independence to the West German government. In July 1951, they agreed to end the state of war with West Germany, even though no all-German state existed with which to contract a peace treaty.

On May 5, 1955, the three western powers issued a carefully worded diplomatic note that accorded the "full authority of a sovereign state" to the West German government. The note preserved a diplomatic subtlety. By extending the "authority of a sovereign state" rather than simply recognizing the Federal Republic as a

[June 17, 1953] "The tanks came in and ran the people back. None of that happened in the American sector or around where we were. They did confine us to the air base.... The Army was on alert throughout the city."

Private James Bourk, U.S. Air Force, 1951–1954

"*All politicians had to land either in Tempelhof or in Tegel with a military aircraft. They could not come with the Bundeswehr [German army] or any kind of German aircraft. They had to take one of the allied aircraft. . . . This is the only way they could enter Berlin. To the Russians, it was illegal for those people to be even in Berlin.*"

Helga Mellmann, Berliner

After the death of Soviet leader Josef Stalin on March 5, 1953, Russians and East Germans placed flowers at the Russian War Memorial, located in the British sector of West Berlin. Despite the Cold War, the memorial continued to attract visitors, including American military.

German Chancellor Konrad Adenauer was welcomed at Tempelhof on April 26, 1955, by Col. Wesley H. Vernon. The chancellor and his economic cabinet travelled to Berlin to discuss steps for a five-year plan for social and economic development of the city.

sovereign state, the allies retained the right to negotiate a final peace treaty officially ending World War II. Until that treaty was signed, the western allies retained the right to remain in Berlin.

On May 6, the Federal Republic joined the NATO alliance and began to organize a new military force. At the same time, the functions of the High Commission for Germany ended, replaced by allied diplomatic recognition of the Federal Republic of Germany. In addition, the military occupation ended for western troops; from that date, they remained in the country by invitation of the West German government as a part of the NATO arrangements for mutual defense. However, because of Berlin's special status, allied troops remained in the city as occupying and protecting forces, and West Berlin continued to pay the costs of the American military presence in the city.

Confronted with the rearmament of West Germany and its inclusion in NATO, the Soviet Union extended full diplomatic recognition to the eastern German Democratic Republic in October 1955 and incorporated it into the Eastern European counter-alliance, the Warsaw Pact.

Even after extension of sovereignty to the Federal Republic of Germany and the German Democratic Republic, Berlin remained a four-power city. The authority of the wartime allies survived in Berlin as a vestige of the alliance that had broken down along East-West lines.

The West German government had no legal status in Berlin, although it maintained close polit-ical and economic ties with the city. With the approval of the three western powers, the West Berlin municipal council systematically adopted legislation passed in the Federal Republic and received much of its budget from the federal government in Bonn.

Because Soviet and East German authorities controlled the 100-mile passage between West Germany and Berlin, travel to the city remained subject to their regulation and vulnerable to harassment. Officials from the government in Bonn had to travel to Berlin in allied military aircraft because the Soviet Union could deny them passage by land. In Berlin, traffic flowed almost unrestricted through 80 official control points along the sector border between the eastern and western halves of the city.

Berliners and American Soldiers

As much as any official negotiations, the Berlin airlift transformed the American military into protectors rather than occupiers. During the 1950s, a new relationship took hold between the citizens of West Berlin and American soldiers and airmen. To show its gratitude, the West Berlin city government planned a memorial to those who had died serving in the airlift. Dedicated on July 10, 1951, it became the site of annual commemorations of the airlift and expressions of German-American friendship.

GERMAN DEMOCRATIC REPUBLIC

• Berlin

FEDERAL REPUBLIC OF GERMANY

• Bonn

The Airlift Memorial (Luftbrücke Denkmal) at Tempelhof, dedicated July 10, 1951, symbolized the bond between Americans and Berliners. The design of the soaring 63-foot high cast-concrete structure represents a broken bridge and the three air corridors. A similar memorial at Rhein-Main air base near Frankfurt, Germany, represents the other end of the Luftbrücke (air bridge).

The Airlift Memorial was the site of ceremonies, including this one July 10, 1955. Its base is inscribed with the names of the men killed participating in the airlift.

"To me, the airlift was the turning point in West Berliners' perception of Americans. From then on, we regarded them as friends and benefactors rather than as conquerors."

Anonymous Berliner

The American military expanded contacts between Berliners and the soldiers serving in the city. The Army band performed concerts for the public. The AFN and RIAS broadcast entertainment and news programs. RIAS added a short-wave transmitter in 1951 and a new 300,000-watt transmitter in 1953. During the June 17 uprisings, hundreds of Germans from the eastern sector and zone brought eyewitness testimony to the station's studios in West Berlin. The RIAS broadcasts of reports from the streets dismayed the East German government, and RIAS became a focus of its anti-western propaganda.

In the mid-1950s, the German Youth Activity clubs, discontinued because of limited funds only a few years earlier, enjoyed a revival. American servicemen participated in club activities and sponsored Thanksgiving dinners and Christmas parties for local children. In *Operation Kinderlift*, the U.S. Army and Air Force cooperated with Berlin and West German authorities to treat thousands of refugee children. Each summer the services flew children to West Germany for month-long vacations in German and American homes and in youth camps established by the United States military.

Increasingly, the disparity between life in the West and life in the East led thousands of East Germans to leave their homes and travel to West Berlin. After the East German authorities closed the border between the eastern and western halves of the nation in May 1952, West Berlin became the last remaining exit point. From there, refugees could travel safely by air to West Germany and greater political and economic

Airmen joined members of the Tempelhof German Youth Activities Club for Thanksgiving dinner in 1955.

"We used to go to some of the local taverns.... I can remember one old gentleman by the name of Walter Winkel. He had a small bar not too far from Tempelhof. A buddy of mine, Jim Murray, from Biloxi, Mississippi—we'd go down there and sit and talk. They couldn't understand us and we couldn't understand them, but we seemed to have a nice relationship."

*Private James Bourk,
U.S. Air Force, 1951–1954*

American soldiers distributed food and Christmas gifts to Berliners from the back of a truck in 1951.

The 298th U.S. Army band performed in a refugee camp in 1954.

The U.S. Army 6th Infantry Regiment received a brown bear, symbol of Berlin, as a gift from the city on Armed Forces Day, May 1957. The unit later delivered the bear to the National Zoo in Washington, D.C.

1945
1946
1947
1948
1949
1950
1951
1952
1953
1954
1955
1956
1957
1958
1959
1960
1961
1962
1963
1964
1965
1966
1967
1968
1969
1970
1971
1972
1973
1974
1975
1976
1977
1978
1979
1980
1981
1982
1983
1984
1985
1986
1987
1988
1989
1990
1991
1992
1993
1994

opportunity. About 119,000 passed through West Berlin in 1952, and over 300,000 in 1953, the year of the June 17 uprisings. Inner-city traffic with East Berlin remained relatively free, and air transport to the West bypassed East German and Russian restrictions. Escape remained possible.

In 1956, the German Democratic Republic passed a law that declared Republikflucht (fleeing the republic) a crime, punishable with a three-year prison sentence. The East Germans also cleared a 3-mile strip along their 860-mile border with West Germany, where they applied stringent security measures. Neither the legislation nor the increased dangers in passing the frontier stemmed the flow of refugees. Total emigration from East to West Germany exceeded 178,000 annually between 1952 and 1959.

Those fleeing included the most educated, the most productive, the most employable members of East German society: over 100,000 farmers and farm workers; 4,500 medical doctors and dentists; 800 lawyers, judges, notaries, and state attorneys; over 17,000 teachers and as many engineers and technicians. Approximately half of the refugees were under 25 years old. By the end of the decade, nearly 4 million East Germans, over 20 percent of East Germany's 1945 population, had fled to the West. The loss of education, talent, and initiative from the flight of so many refugees, to say nothing of the embarrassment that it represented, created the conditions for a new Berlin crisis.

The 287th Military Police included the last horse platoon in the U.S. Army. The MPs conducted their final mounted patrol of the East-West border in Berlin in March 1958, before the unit was permanently retired.

YOU ARE LEAVING
THE AMERICAN SECTOR

ВЫ ВЫЕЗЖАЕТЕ ИЗ
АМЕРИКАНСКОГО СЕКТОРА

VOUS SORTEZ
DU SECTEUR AMERICAIN

SIE VERLASSEN DEN AMERIKANISCHEN SEKTOR

Through the 1950s, sector borders in Berlin, including bridges, were only lightly guarded, making passage relatively easy.

Crisis in Berlin
1958–1962

The Ultimatum

Late in 1958, Soviet Premier Nikita Khrushchev initiated the most serious challenge to the status of Berlin since the blockade. On November 10, Khrushchev declared that the wartime agreements that placed the occupying armies in Berlin were no longer valid, and he demanded a new solution to the status of the city. Seventeen days later, he sent an ultimatum to the United States, Great Britain, France, and the Federal Republic of Germany.

Khrushchev's diplomatic note of November 27 demanded that West Berlin become a demilitarized free city within six months. He insisted that the four powers end the occupation of Berlin and that the western powers withdraw their garrisons. Short of this solution, Khrushchev declared, the Soviet Union would turn over its authority in Berlin—and control of all access to the city—to the German Democratic Republic.

The Crisis Prolonged

If implemented, Khrushchev's ultimatum would force the West to abandon Berlin and to recognize the German Democratic Republic as a second German state. The western powers rejected the

ultimatum, but their response concealed some ambivalence. None of the western leaders favored abandoning Berlin, but they were not prepared to risk nuclear war, so they searched for some accommodation. In the negotiations that followed

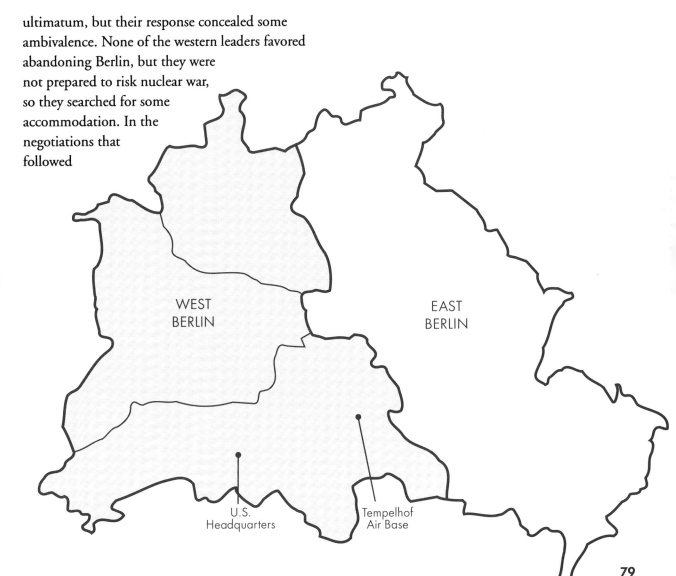

WEST BERLIN

EAST BERLIN

U.S. Headquarters

Tempelhof Air Base

Brandenburg Gate

Khrushchev's challenge, West German leaders opposed recognizing the East German government as a legitimate representative of any part of the German nation. Efforts to defuse the Berlin crisis through negotiations foundered.

As Khrushchev's six-month deadline approached, the foreign ministers from the United States, France, Great Britain, and the Soviet Union convened in Geneva in May 1959. The deadline passed and discussions continued into the summer, even though the diplomats had reached no settlement. The status quo remained the safest refuge. During the Geneva negotiations, the Soviet Union acknowledged the rights of the three western powers in Berlin, including their military presence, pending a formal settlement of World War II with Germany. At President Eisenhower's personal invitation, Khrushchev visited the United States in September 1959. No solution for Berlin resulted, but the Khrushchev visit did produce plans for a summit meeting of the leaders in May 1960.

Just before the summit meeting opened, the Soviet Union shot down an American U-2 spy plane as it flew over Soviet air space, and the level of tension increased. The resulting acrimony aborted the Geneva summit after one day. Within a week, Khrushchev again threatened a separate treaty between the Soviet Union and the East German government. He warned the Western European nations that the presence

"They were even buzzing our aircraft in the corridors. It was part of the harassment techniques they were practicing on us. There were times that we flew with the military transport to Berlin from the Wiesbaden Airfield . . . [and] we had parachutes on. Whether that was overly cautious, I don't know, but it emphasized the threat."

Louis Brettschneider, civilian employee of the U.S. Army

An honor guard sentry stands at the entrance to the U.S. Headquarters in Berlin on Clayallee.

Army Chief of Staff Gen. Maxwell Taylor reviewed troops at Tempelhof air base on May Day, 1959.

Gen. Lucius D. Clay, the American commander during the airlift, visited Berlin on the tenth anniversary of the airlift and laid a wreath at the Airlift Memorial at Tempelhof air base.

of American nuclear weapons in Europe exposed them to annihilation if the crisis came to war.

While the diplomats negotiated, Soviet and East German soldiers harassed vehicles en route to Berlin. They applied restrictions on transit sporadically throughout the extended negotiations. Soviet fighters buzzed allied military aircraft flying to Berlin. Soviet officials imposed new restrictions on the altitude of flights across the corridors. Border officials slowed barge traffic with inspections and controls.

Allied troop strength in Berlin—fewer than 7,000 Americans, 3,000 British, and 1,500 French—was no match for the six divisions of Soviet troops supported by additional East German units stationed around the city. Officers and troops of the Berlin Command understood the symbolic significance of their presence in the city, and their activities underscored their readiness.

This double file of infantry returning from a training exercise was a visible and reassuring sign of the American military presence for West Berliners.

U.S. soldiers practice with rifles on the grounds of McNair Barracks.

The Berlin Command stepped up its normal target range activity and training in hand-to-hand combat.

Army engineers completed a new urban warfare training area in the Lichterfelde district, and U.S. Army units began using it in 1959.

"In May of 1961, they had an East German May Day Parade where they paraded all their equipment and I, being somewhat naive, took my simple Ansco camera over and photographed everything they had. And then I found out later that the intelligence community had been reluctant to do that because they were afraid people would get arrested. I did it out of absolute ignorance. I just did it, and no one said anything to me."

Lynn Hansen, Fulbright student

Open houses at Tempelhof air base and McNair Barracks (shown here) became annual events. Berliners from eastern and western sectors came to see this display (May 1959) of the military equipment used to defend West Berlin's independence.

1945
1946
1947
1948
1949
1950
1951
1952
1953
1954
1955
1956
1957
1958
1959
1960
1961
1962
1963
1964
1965
1966
1967
1968
1969
1970
1971
1972
1973
1974
1975
1976
1977
1978
1979
1980
1981
1982
1983
1984
1985
1986
1987
1988
1989
1990
1991
1992
1993
1994

Summer 1961

In June 1961, at a meeting in Vienna with the new American president, John F. Kennedy, Khrushchev again demanded a German peace treaty, recognition of the East German state, the end of allied occupation rights in Berlin, and West Berlin's conversion to a free city within East Germany, undefended by western military units. Khrushchev again threatened to sign a separate peace treaty with the German Democratic Republic on January 1, 1962, if the four powers had not reached a satisfactory solution by then. At that time, he would turn over full control of Berlin to the East Germans.

Kennedy returned to the United States sobered by Khrushchev's demands. He requested that Congress appropriate an additional $3 billion for defense spending, and he doubled draft quotas to expand the Army.

The crisis atmosphere surrounding Berlin increased East German emigration to the West. With the frontier between East and West Germany sealed, Berlin remained the only easy opening to migration. Conscious that the opportunity might be fleeting, 152,000 East Germans escaped to West Berlin in 1960. Early in 1961, tens of thousands more streamed into West Berlin.

Throughout the summer of 1961, East Germany's political leaders publicly denounced the migration as "filthy man-trade," "filthy head-hunting," and "filthy slave trading." They protested that West German authorities, monopoly capitalists, and American spy centers invested large sums of money to entice East Germans to emigrate. Nothing stopped the exodus.

At the beginning of August, the East Germans increased the number of troops patrolling their border to six times the previous strength. They arrested one of every two Germans seeking asylum in West Berlin, but still a record-breaking 10,419 refugees escaped between July 29 and August 4. On August 11, newspapers in West Berlin reported that East German authorities had met that morning; the papers speculated that the authorities had decided to close the border. The news prompted thousands more to escape, pushing the total of refugees in the first 12 days of August over 45,000.

WILL AMERICANS FIGHT FOR BERLIN?

Q. "Do you think we should keep American forces in Berlin—along with British and French forces—even at the risk of war?"

Yes, should	82%
No, should not	7%
No opinion	11%

Q. "If Communist East Germany closes all roads to Berlin and does not permit planes to land in Berlin, do you think the U.S. and its allies should or should not try to fight their way into Berlin?"

Should fight	71%
Should not	15%
No opinion	14%

Excerpts from a Gallup Poll, printed in *U.S. News and World Report*, August 14, 1961

"Many people worked in the West—earned hard currency—and they commuted back and forth. And they didn't spend their money in the East. They would buy their milk, their bread, flour, staples, in East Berlin, but they would buy all the others in the West. Many professionals left. They just took the subway. . . . That something would happen or had to happen was almost clear."

Renate Semler, Berliner

U.S. Berlin Command troops
participate in an alert drill.

The Wall

Under cover of darkness, between midnight and 2:00 A.M. on Sunday, August 13, 1961, East Germany acted. An estimated 40,000 heavily armed soldiers and police—with tanks, armored cars, personnel carriers, trucks with water cannon, and other military vehicles in support—lined the sector border between East and West Berlin. They felled trees across streets, cut streetcar tracks and bent them back to form bumpers, tore up paving stones, dug trenches across parks and plazas, installed cement posts, and strung coils of barbed wire.

By morning, the East German regime had its solution in place: a barrier along the entire border between West and East Berlin. Of the 80 crossing points used between the two halves of the city during the 1950s, the East Germans left only 13 open, all controlled by armed East German guards. The regime's answer to the exodus of its citizens was the Berlin Wall.

> *"Almost like the Middle Ages, to build a wall was incredible."*
>
> *Renate Semler, Berliner*

The Wall was initially constructed of barbed wire strung between concrete posts.

The Wall closed off streets, including this street between the French and the Soviet sectors.

To prevent escapes, East Germans bricked up windows in buildings near the border, including windows of this house along Bernauerstrasse.

Reactions to the Wall

Berliners were stunned by the construction of the Wall. Overnight they had been cut off from family, friends, and coworkers. East German border guards stopped the 53,000 East Berliners employed in West Berlin from traveling to work. A driver for a West Berlin firm, too drunk to return to East Berlin on Saturday, August 12, decided when he awoke Sunday morning that he had been lucky. No West Berliners were allowed to pass through the Wall. Buildings that straddled the border were sealed. Even a Huguenot cemetery with entrances on each side of the sector border was closed off, and West Berliners were not allowed to visit family graves in East Berlin.

West Berliners were also incensed. In the first ten days, many took to the streets, and a crowd assembled menacingly at the Brandenburg Gate. On August 17, protesters threatened to vent their anger by attacking the Russian soldiers stationed as an honor guard at the Soviet War Memorial, located in the British sector. British troops had to surround the memorial with barbed wire to protect the Russians from the hostile crowd.

Within days, construction workers, guarded by East German soldiers, built a second, sturdier barrier behind the first, laying concrete blocks, stringing additional barbed wire, and erecting watch towers. The East Germans installed a machine gun at the top of the Brandenburg Gate. Soldiers on guard along the Wall had orders to shoot anyone trying to escape.

West Berliners climbed up to look over the Wall to deserted streets in East Berlin.

This woman waves to relatives across the Wall in the Bernauerstrasse area.

Within weeks, East Germans constructed a second barrier of concrete blocks behind the first barrier of concrete posts and barbed wire.

The American Response

The reaction of the United States' government to the Wall was limited to rhetoric and military mobilization. President Kennedy protested but took no steps to remove the Wall, which the East Germans had carefully set up on their side of the sector border. Kennedy ordered the reinforcement of the American military presence in Berlin, and he dispatched Vice President Lyndon B. Johnson and General Clay to the city.

Johnson and Clay arrived on August 19. The next day, the U.S. Army sent the 1st Battle Group, 18th Infantry (Reinforced) across the autobahn from Helmstedt in West Germany to Berlin. The 1,500-man battle group arrived on the afternoon of August 20 and paraded through the streets for review by Vice President Johnson and General Clay.

Berliners were angry and confused by the American response because none of the measures taken challenged the physical reality of the Wall. They were deeply troubled that 29 miles of barbed wire and cement block brutally divided their city. The barrier also encircled the city for an additional 70 miles, shutting West Berlin off from the East German countryside. Berliners found the barrier repugnant, an ugly scar in their daily landscape. The realization that the western powers were unwilling to risk a world war to remove the Wall sobered and troubled them.

West Berliners took their greatest reassurance from President Kennedy's selection of Lucius

The barrier built by the East Germans ringed West Berlin, cutting it off from the countryside. East German police patrolled the border with dogs.

"At first, there was almost an inability to understand why ... why the Americans, our friends, and the British—why nobody does anything. ... There were speculations: This was maybe an arrangement, maybe they knew in advance and they didn't want to have a conflict. ... Now we were this little island. ... Now we didn't even have the other half of the city."

Renate Semler, Berliner

"During the period of the Wall being built, we were never sure what was going to happen in Berlin. I had my wife and young son with me, and my wife was pregnant, and we had suitcases packed all the time. We had C-rations available to us in case there was another blockade.... It couldn't have lasted much more than a week where we actually dressed in fatigues and there was this sort of touch-and-go thing and we were advised to stay near a telephone to find out whether a decision had been made to get our families out. I think the overall decision was that we weren't going to panic by sending families out. We were going to demonstrate resoluteness and self-confidence by staying."

Lieutenant Lynn Hansen,
U.S. Air Force, Berlin, 1961–1963

Children peering over the Wall could see the area cleared as a no-man's zone.

Clay to accompany Vice President Johnson to Berlin. They remembered Clay with affection for his steadfastness during the blockade. After Clay and Johnson had returned to Washington to report to the president, Kennedy appointed Clay as his personal envoy to Berlin. Clay flew back to Berlin in mid-September.

Confrontations at the Wall

Even before Clay's return to Berlin, the beginnings of a tense confrontation were developing. Within days after the Wall went up, East Germans reduced the number of points of passage from 13 to 7 street crossings and 1 rail crossing. On August 22, they announced that only the crossing at Friedrichstrasse in the American sector would be open for foreigners, including members of the American forces, to enter East Berlin. The following day, U.S. Army military police established an ad hoc station at the Friedrichstrasse control point to monitor traffic and to watch for problems.

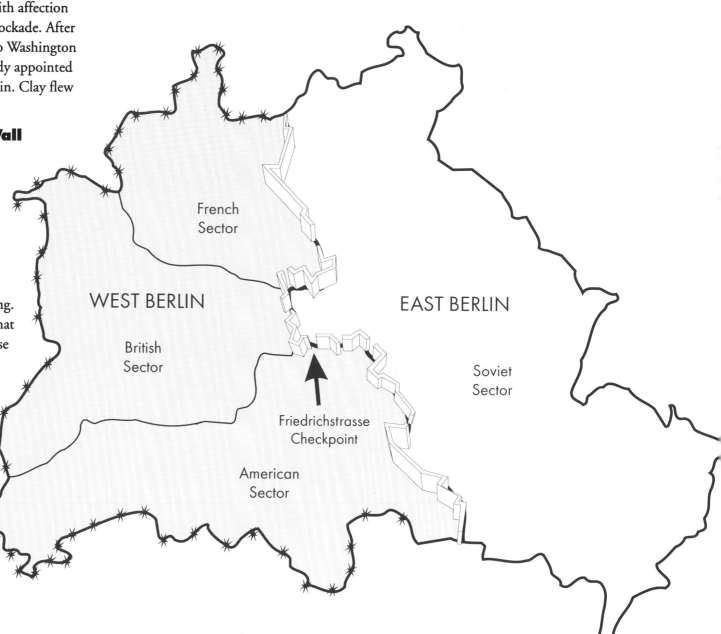

American Military Police maintained communications with their headquarters from their post on the West Berlin side of Wilhelmstrasse during the tense days of August 1961.

During August 1961, American forces patrolled the border crossing at Friedrichstrasse in a jeep mounted with a 30-caliber machine gun.

By agreement and precedent, members of the military mission of any of the four occupying powers in Berlin moved freely about the city. Uniformed military passed without inspection of their identification papers. Civilians in vehicles with allied military license plates had the same privilege. On August 30, East Germans challenged that privilege. They detained an American military vehicle trying to enter East Berlin at Friedrichstrasse. The U.S. commander dispatched an armored unit with tanks to the sector border. The East Germans gave way and released the vehicle and its occupants, and the American tanks retired. The incident showed, however, the potential for confrontation.

Following the confrontation on August 30, U.S. Army military police requisitioned space on the Friedrichstrasse so they could post sentries to monitor the checkpoint more regularly. They had never needed such an installation before because their monitoring patrols had been intermittent. They set up a temporary trailer in front of the apartment at 207 Friedrichstrasse. They used the apartment as an office and a desk inside the trailer as the checkpoint. On the north end of the trailer, the side closest to the Wall, they positioned sandbags to form a protective bunker for riflemen.

The military police also oversaw the checkpoints at either end of the autobahn that ran through East German territory to Berlin, points Alfa and Bravo. Because the position at Friedrichstrasse was the third control point under their command, the sentries put a wooden

Jeeps on patrol near the sector border had to make a U-turn when they reached the newly constructed Wall.

In the tense weeks after the Wall was erected, East German police positioned water trucks near the Friedrichstrasse border checkpoint to spray water on people who got too close to the border or on crowds that got too large.

1945
1946
1947
1948
1949
1950
1951
1952
1953
1954
1955
1956
1957
1958
1959
1960
1961
1962
1963
1964
1965
1966
1967
1968
1969
1970
1971
1972
1973
1974
1975
1976
1977
1978
1979
1980
1981
1982
1983
1984
1985
1986
1987
1988
1989
1990
1991
1992
1993
1994

sign over the door of the apartment with the two-line inscription: "U.S. Army/Checkpoint Charlie." Within weeks, the name became known worldwide as a focal point of Cold War tensions in Berlin.

The American decisionmakers in Berlin; presidential envoy Lucius Clay; U.S. Commander, Berlin, Major General Albert Watson, 2d; and the senior State Department representative in Berlin, Allan Lightner, Jr., wanted to use every occasion possible to assert American prerogatives in the city. They saw the incident at Friedrichstrasse as presenting a double opportunity. First, they wanted to counter any suggestion that the American military command accepted the authority of the East German police, officials of a government that the United States did not recognize as legitimate. Second, they saw a way to expose the Soviet ruse that the East German regime was in charge of events surrounding the construction of the Wall and the restrictions on traffic.

On October 22, 1961, Lightner tried to cross to East Berlin at Checkpoint Charlie in an appropriately licensed vehicle. When he refused to show his credentials, the East Germans denied him passage. Lightner returned to the American side and picked up an escort of military police who accompanied his car through the checkpoint without a second challenge.

The Americans sent officials on similar excursions in the following days. Each time they faced an initial obstruction, but no challenge when they returned with an armed escort.

On October 26, the U.S. Army moved tanks to positions at Checkpoint Charlie to emphasize the right of free access. The next afternoon, Soviet tanks moved into position on the eastern side of the sector border. For the next 24 hours, tension remained high, but American military and diplomatic travelers moved without restriction through the checkpoint, and Soviet and American tanks in the street faced one another across the Wall.

General Clay called a news conference while the atmosphere was still tense and announced:

> *The fiction that it was the East Germans who were responsible for trying to prevent allied access to East Berlin is now destroyed. The fact that Soviet tanks appeared on the scene proves that the harassments . . . taking place at Friedrichstrasse were not those of the self-styled East German government but ordered by its Soviet masters.*

Tensions subsided near noon on October 28, when both the Soviet and American forces withdrew to staging areas farther from the border. The confrontation had served its purpose. Challenges to the free movement of military personnel occurred during the next several years, but the American leaders on site had clearly reaffirmed the allied prerogative of free

East German police in a personnel carrier watched the street and the Wall near Heinrich Heine Strasse, while a small child in the window watched the police.

Confrontation of American and Soviet tanks, October 1961

1945
1946
1947
1948
1949
1950
1951
1952
1953
1954
1955
1956
1957
1958
1959
1960
1961
1962
1963
1964
1965
1966
1967
1968
1969
1970
1971
1972
1973
1974
1975
1976
1977
1978
1979
1980
1981
1982
1983
1984
1985
1986
1987
1988
1989
1990
1991
1992
1993
1994

access to East Berlin and had established the fact that the Soviets, not the East Germans, determined who passed the border.

Clay and American Rights

As a retired general, Clay had no military authority. He had, however, the moral authority of his tenure as commander in Berlin between 1945 and 1949. His understanding of the legal rights and precedents affecting the American position in Berlin made him particularly sensitive to the challenges that the East Germans and the Soviets posed. His decisive personality, his stature as the successful commander of the airlift, and his position as a special advisor to the president gave him the authority he needed.

Clay asserted American prerogatives wherever they were challenged. He insisted that these rights were grounded legally in the wartime diplomatic arrangements designating Berlin as a four-power city. He saw the Wall as a unilateral attempt to invalidate allied rights in Berlin. Even before the October confrontation at Checkpoint Charlie he had taken opportunities to exercise those rights. These incidents did not capture international headlines, but they were just as reassuring to the West Berliners as any other action the American government undertook.

Shortly after his return to Berlin as presidential envoy, for example, Clay flew by helicopter to the tiny enclave of Steinstücken, a community of only a few hundred residents. Traditionally a part of Zehlendorf, a district in the American sector of Berlin, Steinstücken was physically separated from the main area of West Berlin by a 1,200-yard strip of ground that was East German territory. In the 1950s, the Soviets had tried to incorporate the enclave into East Germany, but, after a brief confrontation, conceded American authority.

When Clay visited the area, now isolated by the barrier around Berlin, the East Germans and the Soviet military protested the violation of East German air space. A week later, Clay sent a helicopter to Steinstücken to pick up refugees who had reached the village. He also began rotating American military police by helicopter to a permanent station in the community. The Soviets ringed Steinstücken with barbed wire but took no other action. The American detachment served Steinstücken until 1972, when the powers settled the community's status by agreement.

Clay also renewed the movement of small military patrols along the autobahn that ran across East Germany to Berlin. He sent American armored cars to drive the length of the autobahn between Checkpoints Alfa in the west and Bravo just inside the American sector of Berlin. The Soviets protested, but Clay insisted that the right of access to Berlin permitted such patrols.

Before construction of the Wall and the barrier around West Berlin, passage between the American sector and the enclave of Steinstücken was largely unchallenged. The sign on the left directs travelers to Checkpoint Bravo, the easternmost point on the autobahn through East Germany.

ECK POINT
BRAVO

←

YOU ARE LEAVING
THE
AMERICAN SECTOR
SIE VERLASSEN DEN
AMERIKANISCHEN
SEKTOR

Zum Ortsteil
Steinstücken
Zugang nur mit
besonderer Genehmigung

1945
1946
1947
1948
1949
1950
1951
1952
1953
1954
1955
1956
1957
1958
1959
1960
1961
1962
1963
1964
1965
1966
1967
1968
1969
1970
1971
1972
1973
1974
1975
1976
1977
1978
1979
1980
1981
1982
1983
1984
1985
1986
1987
1988
1989
1990
1991
1992
1993
1994

Through all of the probing, no one was quite sure what the Soviets would do if provoked. People feared another blockade. The United States had taken steps to prepare for that possibility. President Kennedy had activated United States reserve forces in September and moved many of them to forward positions in Western Europe. He also authorized preparation for an airlift if necessary. Under the code name *Operation Bamboo Tree*, U.S. Army engineers supervised hurried construction and the installation of electronic navigation devices at airfields in West Berlin. Tegel airfield in the French sector received much of the construction because its 7,800-foot runways were long enough to accommodate jet transport aircraft.

This aerial view of the Wall shows two barriers and the cleared strip between them, November 1961.

"I got a call from the Air Force, 'Come to a meeting.' I believe it was in October '61. It was a top-secret meeting. They said the Russians were going to close off the corridor [to Berlin] and we have to put in NAVAIDS [navigational aids] for new airlifts.

"I said, 'That's good, now what's the time frame on all this?' They said, 'We need it by New Years.' The first thing was a building for the tower... a high tower atop the hangar at Tempelhof.... I asked them if they were serious [about the time frame]. They said, 'Oh, absolutely. Everybody is in this, and we have a piece of paper from [Secretary of Defense Robert] McNamara: 'No administrative orders or procedures can stand in the way of the proper completion of this task.' That gives you quite a bit of authority."

Saul Fraint, retired civilian employee of the U.S. Army

East Germans continued to reinforce the Wall. This view of a street in the French sector shows how the Wall cut public transportation routes, including the streetcar tracks.

[At Tegel, the Air Force installed stroboscopic lights on the airfield to guide pilots even in inclement weather.]

"We worked, and the contractors worked, in Berlin right around the clock. They worked through Christmas, which is very unusual. Nobody told the German contractors in Berlin specifically what we were about, but everyone was aware. The Wall had been built, tension was very high, and you didn't have to explain things to them.

"It was a very cold winter, extremely low temperatures. We had to lay some cable at Tegel, and almost all cable in those days was plastic covered, the outer coat is plastic if the insulation isn't. Plastic tends to become brittle at very low temperatures and of course even if you get hairline cracks, then the insulation value is down to naught because the moisture penetrates. These were direct burial cables laid out on the airfields, so they had to be very careful. The cable was heated until it became pliable enough to be laid without danger of cracking. Special precautions had to be taken. You needed people out there who were careful.

"We were up at the main Siemens office in Berlin, explaining what we had to have done. This had to be done on Christmas Day, that was our schedule. The director was there, surrounded by his assistants, and Mr. Fraint explained [in German] exactly what had to be done and why. We needed people out there who would insure that the work was done properly despite the weather conditions. The director looked around and said, 'Okay, Mr. Fraint, I understand. I will be there.' Then he turned to look at his guys and he said, 'Who will accompany me?'

"That's the kind of cooperation we got there. . . . Everybody, everybody recognized that it might be a life-and-death issue whether or not Berlin could be supplied by air. So the cooperation of the contractors was marvelous."

Louis Brettschneider, civilian employee of the U.S. Army

The Harshness of the Wall

As fall turned to winter, the reality of the Wall seemed even harsher. The Wall had sliced Berlin in two. Attempts to leave East Germany through Berlin continued, but at a very reduced rate. Even in the first days after the Wall was erected, some people died jumping from buildings on the border. The East German border guards shot others trying to flee.

One of the early shooting victims was Dieter Wohlfahrt, a 20-year-old student at West Berlin's Technical University. Wohlfahrt had brought his fiancée over from East Berlin by using false identity papers; on the night of December 9, 1961, he planned to rescue her mother. They met at a farm house on the western edge of the city just beyond the border between East German territory and the British sector. Wohlfahrt cut through the first of three barbed wire barriers blocking the way to West Berlin. As he crawled toward the second barrier, search lights came on, and the guards shot and seriously wounded him. Someone must have informed, because guards appeared immediately at the farm house to arrest the mother. The East Germans brandished their weapons at the West German police and the British soldiers on the scene. The westerners could not move to help Wohlfahrt as he lay dying in the field. After two hours, a truck came to haul his body away.

The Wall made painfully public the willingness of the East German regime to kill its own citizens rather than let them escape. West Berliners observed 50 victims shot by East German

West Berliners spontaneously erected memorials to people who died trying to reach the West. Ida Siekmann jumped to her death August 22, 1961, one day before her 60th birthday.

East German police peered menacingly over the Wall.

1945
1946
1947
1948
1949
1950
1951
1952
1953
1954
1955
1956
1957
1958
1959
1960
1961
1962
1963
1964
1965
1966
1967
1968
1969
1970
1971
1972
1973
1974
1975
1976
1977
1978
1979
1980
1981
1982
1983
1984
1985
1986
1987
1988
1989
1990
1991
1992
1993
1994

guards in the first year of the Wall's existence. Escapes dropped from the hundreds of thousands a year to just 12,000 in the first year after the Wall's construction, and to fewer in subsequent years.

Each time refugees found an escape route, the East Germans took measures to close it. East German frogmen fitted waterways with obstructing nets and mines. Under supervision of East German police, workers bricked up windows and entrances to buildings on the border. At times, entire structures were razed. Work on the Wall continued.

The East Germans claimed that they had built the Wall because the western powers and West Germany had planned to launch a military offensive into East Germany through Berlin.

They called it the Friedensmauer (Wall of Peace), alleging that it had prevented the invasion. The six-to-one ratio of forces in the Soviets' favor made such an attack improbable, if not absurd. They did not explain why the barriers and the killing zone hindered access to the Wall only from the eastern side.

At the end of 1961, the atmosphere in Berlin was strained and the mood somber. The Wall had stopped the mass exodus of Germans to the West, but it was not clear that the crisis was over. The Soviets could still impose another blockade. Separated by the Wall, families celebrated the Christmas holidays apart. No one knew how Berliners would live with the Wall.

Aerial view of the
Brandenburg Gate,
November 1961

Enduring the Wall
1962–1973

The construction of the Wall had provoked no armed combat by January 1962, but Berlin remained tense, not sure that the prospect of war had passed. Over the next six months, life in West Berlin gradually returned to a semblance of calm. Berliners, who thought of themselves as *Krisenprofis* or "crisis professionals," began to adjust to an uncomfortable new normality, life in a physically divided city.

Mixed Results

The East German government needed the Wall in Berlin to stop its loss of people. Measured against that objective, the Wall succeeded. Of the 12,300 who fled to West Berlin in the first year after the Wall went up, one-third escaped in the first two months. Thereafter, what had been a flood of refugees became a trickle.

The East German and Soviet leaders also hoped that the Wall could isolate West Berlin and deprive it of its economic and moral support. Measured against that objective, the Wall failed.

The East Germans removed the planks on bridges between the sectors to prevent cars from driving at high speed and ramming through the gate on the east side.

Brandenburg Gate in 1962

1945
1946
1947
1948
1949
1950
1951
1952
1953
1954
1955
1956
1957
1958
1959
1960
1961
1962
1963
1964
1965
1966
1967
1968
1969
1970
1971
1972
1973
1974
1975
1976
1977
1978
1979
1980
1981
1982
1983
1984
1985
1986
1987
1988
1989
1990
1991
1992
1993
1994

The Economy and the Wall

West Berlin's economy suffered a shock when the Wall cut off 53,000 East Berliners from their jobs in West Berlin. Even by mid-1962, West Berlin had only 10,000 unemployed workers to fill 35,000 available jobs. To encourage people to relocate, the city established bureaus to provide information on job possibilities and places to live. Newcomers also received $125 to offset moving expenses.

During the first four months of the crisis, about 15,000 permanent residents of West Berlin resettled to West Germany, taking their savings with them. West Berlin's economy then had to contend with this loss of personal savings, and thus of the investment capital that could stimulate economic activity. By the spring, however, more Germans moved each month to West Berlin than left. By summer, the level of personal savings had surpassed pre-Wall totals, and business orders had increased 4 percent over the previous year. To encourage continued investment in Berlin, the West German government supported the city with tax advantages for businesses and substantial subsidies to the city administration.

The willingness of West Berliners to contribute to relief campaigns for others demonstrates that their morale had improved after the initial shock of the Wall. In February 1962, devastating floods hit Hamburg. West Berlin's citizens contributed over 5 million deutschmarks ($1.25 million) to the national collection to help flood victims. The money may have come in large

In the 1960s, rubble from war-damaged buildings still remained in Berlin. Workers cleared this building site near the Berlin Hilton Hotel.

A new tower stands next to the damaged remains of the Kaiser Wilhelm Memorial Church amid other new buildings reflecting growing prosperity.

"*The university, probably with funds from the Federal Republic in Bonn, arranged a bus trip to Berlin for us. They showed this group of American students both West and East Berlin. The big new Mercedes-Benz building near the Kaiser Wilhelm Gedächtniskirche contrasted with the dreariness of East Berlin. Even where the East German government was doing construction, trying to impress outsiders, I don't think they fooled too many people.*"

Martin Reuss, American exchange student in Germany, 1965

1945
1946
1947
1948
1949
1950
1951
1952
1953
1954
1955
1956
1957
1958
1959
1960
1961
1962
1963
1964
1965
1966
1967
1968
1969
1970
1971
1972
1973
1974
1975
1976
1977
1978
1979
1980
1981
1982
1983
1984
1985
1986
1987
1988
1989
1990
1991
1992
1993
1994

measure from the 100 marks that all Berliners received as a vacation allowance in the spring of 1962—what they called their "jitter bonus." The self-deprecating humor did not obscure the underlying reality. Berliners recognized that their fortunes, however bad, were better than some.

Clay's Departure

In mid-April of 1962, newspapers in Berlin reported that Lucius Clay would soon return to the United States, and West Berliners became uneasy. Their discomfort increased when reports circulated that the announcement had come as a surprise to Clay himself. Clay had vigorously asserted American rights in the face of the Soviet and East German challenges. He had frustrated East German efforts to curtail American and allied military activities in the city. He had forcefully affirmed the rights of residents of Steinstücken. West Berliners doubted that anyone would protect their interests or understand their situation as well.

To calm public fears, Clay asserted that he could be a more effective advocate for Berlin from the United States than from his position in the city. Berliners remained unconvinced, although they realized that Clay could not stay indefinitely.

Before Clay departed, the West Berlin city government made him a guest of honor at the 1962 May Day celebration, held in the Platz der Republik, near the Brandenburg Gate and the Wall. A crowd of 700,000, one-third of the

Districts of East and West Berlin with the Wall dividing the city

population of Berlin, paid tribute to Clay. The East Germans placed loudspeakers near the Wall and blared their own May Day celebrations into the plaza in an attempt to disrupt the tribute, but they failed. The city government made Clay an honorary citizen, a privilege granted to only one other foreigner in Berlin's long history.

Diplomatic discussions about Berlin took place between the Soviet Union and the United States

On July 4, 1962, after a parade in the Kreuzberg district, a ceremony at the Airlift Memorial honored the United States. Flags from each of the 50 states were presented, and a 50-gun cannonade fired. Street parades and friendship days in each district of the American sector nurtured the German-American bond through the 1960s.

1945
1946
1947
1948
1949
1950
1951
1952
1953
1954
1955
1956
1957
1958
1959
1960
1961
1962
1963
1964
1965
1966
1967
1968
1969
1970
1971
1972
1973
1974
1975
1976
1977
1978
1979
1980
1981
1982
1983
1984
1985
1986
1987
1988
1989
1990
1991
1992
1993
1994

through the spring and summer of 1962. Berliners concluded that, as long as the talks continued, the city faced no immediate crisis. By the end of the first year with the Wall, Berliners felt not optimistic, but fatalistic. The Wall was depressing, and the United States government's toleration of it was troubling, but few could propose acceptable alternatives, and no satisfactory solution appeared imminent.

Victims of the Wall

The Wall and the shoot-to-kill order carried out diligently by the East German border guards became daunting obstacles to escape. From the days immediately following the closing of the border, people died while trying to flee East Germany. Some who jumped from windows of buildings that opened to West Berlin fell to their deaths. In dozens of instances during the first year, observers in West Berlin witnessed refugees shot by East German guards. Dieter Wohlfahrt's death just before Christmas 1961 took place out of public view, in a rural part of the city. Only British troops and West Berlin police looked on helplessly as Wohlfahrt died of the gunshot wounds inflicted by the East German guards.

Other deaths were more public. A few days after the Wall's first anniversary, on August 16, 1962, 18-year-old Peter Fechter tried to escape just 100 yards from Checkpoint Charlie. East German guards shot him in the stomach and the back as he tried to climb the Wall. Left where he fell, Fechter cried for help, but no one on the western side could cross to aid him with-

out escalating the incident. He suffered an hour before he died.

Fechter's death provoked groups of West Berliners to riot against the brutality of the East German guards. Protesters stoned buses carrying Soviet troops to relieve guards at their war memorial in the British sector. Soviet military commanders ordered armored personnel carriers to transport the guards to the memorial, adding further provocation. After repeated incidents, allied authorities convinced the Soviet military to abandon the armored personnel carriers and to use a crossing point closer to the memorial when rotating the guards.

More enduring than the anger expressed by Berliners were the memorials to those who died at the Wall. Many of them sprang up spontaneously, placed by unknown persons as an expression of grief, both for the fallen and for the plight of the divided city. Some took on the character of enduring remembrances, which Berliners regularly decorated with garlands or flowers.

The East Germans erected guard towers and searchlights to spot people trying to cross the borders.

Mourners laid flowers at a memorial to 18-year-old Peter Fechter, killed in August 1962.

1945
1946
1947
1948
1949
1950
1951
1952
1953
1954
1955
1956
1957
1958
1959
1960
1961
1962
1963
1964
1965
1966
1967
1968
1969
1970
1971
1972
1973
1974
1975
1976
1977
1978
1979
1980
1981
1982
1983
1984
1985
1986
1987
1988
1989
1990
1991
1992
1993
1994

Reinforcing the Wall

Each time someone escaped, either through the Wall or through the barriers that surrounded the rest of West Berlin, the East German authorities took action. Dieter Wohlfahrt had faced three spaced fences of barbed wire strung thickly on 10-foot-high concrete posts in the rural area where he was shot. By the summer of 1962, East German authorities had added a ditch 3 feet deep and 8 feet wide and a barren 30-yard strip of land, cleared of all cover and mined.

Watch towers rose at intervals of about 3,000 feet around West Berlin. Bunkers of earth and logs stood beside the towers. Searchlights swept the area, and East German guards, always in pairs to control one another, patrolled frequently.

Along the Wall that bisected the city, East German soldiers and workers labored continuously. They replaced barbed wire with concrete blocks and set out tank traps that looked like giant concrete jacks arranged in neat rows. At intervals, they spaced 70 concrete pillboxes for machine guns. The second wall, behind the barrier closest to the west, obstructed easy view and prevented western policemen, journalists, and photographers from witnessing or recording the guards shooting escapees.

Behind the first barrier of cement posts and barbed wire, the East Germans erected walls of cement blocks and tank traps.

From guard towers and military vehicles, the East Germans patrolled the border.

"The East Germans never ceased building on that wall. ... The Wall in 1961 [was] an absolutely ugly edifice hastily thrown together, cinder blocks, the mortar thrown in, and not necessarily well-laid, and so it was an eyesore.

"Ten years later, in most places they had changed the nature of the Wall into these prefabricated concrete blocks with a cylinder on top. As it goes, the Wall was still ugly, but it didn't have the same characteristics as this first primitive cement block wall. Whether they did that for political reasons, because it was so ugly, or they did it for construction reasons, that it was a better wall, I am just not sure.

"I used to marvel at the fact that in '71 to '75 you would still see them working on the Wall in various places."

Colonel Lynn Hansen, U.S. Air Force, retired

In areas where there was little room for a series of barriers, the East Germans fortified the border with broken bottles set in concrete, tank traps, and a moatlike ditch.

Kennedy in Berlin

The Wall became the potent symbol of Berlin as an outpost of the Cold War. West German and American spokesmen kept this image before the public. In June 1963, President John F. Kennedy made a trip to Berlin, underscoring the city's role as a beacon of freedom. In a day-long visit, Kennedy walked the streets of the American sector, visited the Berlin Command, reviewed the troops, and delivered several public speeches.

In remarks delivered during his visit to the Schöneberg City Hall, the seat of West Berlin city government, Kennedy acknowledged his hosts, German Chancellor Konrad Adenauer and West Berlin Mayor Willy Brandt. He also recognized a fellow American, retired general Lucius Clay, who had accompanied him to Berlin. Kennedy acclaimed the contributions that each man had made to democracy in Germany, to the will of Berliners to remain free, and to the bond between Berliners and Americans.

Kennedy then paid tribute to the Berliners themselves:

> *Two thousand years ago the proudest boast was "Civis Romanus Sum" [I am a Roman citizen]. Today in the world of freedom the proudest boast is "Ich bin ein Berliner."*
>
> *There are many people in the world who really don't understand, or say they don't, what is the great issue between the free world and the communist world. Let them come to Berlin.*

President John F. Kennedy and West Berlin Mayor Willy Brandt walked the streets, greeting Berliners and American military and their families.

Kennedy signed
autographs near the
Friedrichstrasse
crossing point.

From this viewing stand,
Kennedy looked into East
Berlin at the historic
Brandenburg Gate.

1945
1946
1947
1948
1949
1950
1951
1952
1953
1954
1955
1956
1957
1958
1959
1960
1961
1962
1963
1964
1965
1966
1967
1968
1969
1970
1971
1972
1973
1974
1975
1976
1977
1978
1979
1980
1981
1982
1983
1984
1985
1986
1987
1988
1989
1990
1991
1992
1993
1994

There are some who say that communism is the wave of the future. Let them come to Berlin. There are some who in Europe and elsewhere say, "We can work with the communists." Let them come to Berlin. And there are even a few who say it is true that communism is an evil system, but it permits us to make economic progress. Lasst sie nach Berlin kommen. Let them come to Berlin.

Freedom has many difficulties and democracy is not perfect. But we have never had to put a wall up to keep our people in, to prevent them from leaving us. . . .

What is true of this city is true of Germany—real, lasting peace in Europe can never be assured as long as one German out of four is denied the elementary right of free men, and that is to make a free choice. . . . Freedom is indivisible, and when one man is enslaved, all are not free. When all are free, then we can look forward to that day when this city will be joined as one and this country and this great continent of Europe in a peaceful and hopeful globe. When that day finally comes, as it will, the people of West Berlin can take sober satisfaction in the fact that they were in the front lines for almost two decades.

All free men, wherever they may live, are citizens of Berlin. And therefore, as a free man, I take pride in the words "Ich bin ein Berliner."

Kennedy's rhetoric brought no concrete changes to Berlin, but it affirmed West Berliners' sense of the significance of their plight in a much larger struggle. It boosted their morale. It also won for Kennedy their admiration and devotion.

With military commanders and retired general Lucius Clay at his side, Kennedy addressed the audience at U.S. Headquarters, near the end of his day-long trip to Berlin.

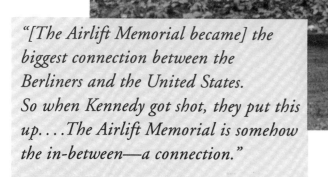

Wir haben einen Freund verloren

"[The Airlift Memorial became] the biggest connection between the Berliners and the United States. So when Kennedy got shot, they put this up....The Airlift Memorial is somehow the in-between—a connection."

Helga Mellmann, Berliner

After the assassination of President Kennedy, Germans laid flowers at the Airlift Memorial and erected a sign reading "We have lost a friend."

1945
1946
1947
1948
1949
1950
1951
1952
1953
1954
1955
1956
1957
1958
1959
1960
1961
1962
1963
1964
1965
1966
1967
1968
1969
1970
1971
1972
1973
1974
1975
1976
1977
1978
1979
1980
1981
1982
1983
1984
1985
1986
1987
1988
1989
1990
1991
1992
1993
1994

Streamlining Command and Support Functions

For West Berliners, the visible evidence of the American commitment to preserving their freedom was the presence of the American troops and their families. To meet the challenge effectively, the American military command continuously reviewed its capacity to respond quickly. The crisis following the August 13 construction of the Wall exposed a complication in the lines of command that had slowed the reaction time of the troops in Berlin.

Before the crisis, responsibility for troop command in Berlin had passed through the U.S. Army, Europe, in Heidelberg. The commander in chief in Heidelberg, General Bruce Clarke, found this cumbersome. To eliminate delays, he reorganized the lines of command on December 1, 1961, subordinating the troop command in Berlin directly to the U.S. Commander, Berlin. To correspond to the new authority, he created the title, Commander, U.S. Army, Berlin, and added it to the other responsibilities held by the U.S. Commander, Berlin. Simultaneously, he redesignated the troop command from Berlin Garrison to U.S. Army, Berlin Brigade.

Late in 1962, the brigade received an important reinforcement when Battery C, 94th Artillery, was assigned to Berlin. This single battery gave the western sectors their only artillery support. Army reorganizations in 1963 augmented the firepower of the Berlin Brigade's tank unit, Company F, 40th Armored. The company received additional tanks to replace two assault gun platoons and added a sixth platoon of tanks to the company. By the end of 1963, Company F had 32 new M60A1 Patton tanks. When the newest equipment arrived, the brigade publicized the modernization and offered rides in the tanks to reporters from West Berlin's newspapers.

The American Guarantee

The machines of war existed only to support the soldiers and the airmen defending the rights and prerogatives that American policymakers sought to maintain. American units practiced urban combat skills in the mock city training area. They received instruction in hand-to-hand fighting and riot control. They guarded Steinstücken. They patrolled the Wall.

The patrols along the Wall generally consisted of three soldiers in alert gear traveling in a jeep fitted with a mounted machine gun. Patrols operated around the clock, each patrol normally covering 16 miles. The soldiers searched for changes in fortifications, observed troop and vehicle movements on the other side, and inspected the crossing points in the Wall to see that warning signs remained readable and in place. Along the way, they exchanged information with West Berlin police in their observation posts and with other U.S. Army patrols.

Posters reminded U.S. military of the importance of their presence in Germany.

Capt. James Graham leads his unit in the Armed Forces Day parade through the American sector, May 1972.

1945
1946
1947
1948
1949
1950
1951
1952
1953
1954
1955
1956
1957
1958
1959
1960
1961
1962
1963
1964
1965
1966
1967
1968
1969
1970
1971
1972
1973
1974
1975
1976
1977
1978
1979
1980
1981
1982
1983
1984
1985
1986
1987
1988
1989
1990
1991
1992
1993
1994

Airmen of the Berlin Command staffed the radar that monitored traffic in the air corridors between Berlin and West Germany. Military and commercial planes in these corridors faced sporadic harassment. Between 1946 and 1964, Soviet fighters attacked 12 U.S. aircraft, leading to the deaths of 36 crew and passengers. During the 1960s, Soviet jets continued to buzz western aircraft. They even dropped metal chaff to disrupt electronic navigational aids. Their threats and harassment did not deter western pilots.

For pilots and soldiers alike, discipline was essential. Pilots could not deviate from their flight plans. Allied and American soldiers could not go beyond their orders, which were to patrol and observe, but not to intervene. They could not cross the border to help escapees, even those who lay mortally wounded within sight of the Wall.

The atmosphere of crisis engendered by the Berlin Wall did not end, but it did slowly wind down. In January 1966, the last of the reinforcement battalions that had rotated to Berlin every 90 days since August 20, 1961, withdrew from Berlin. The Berlin Brigade maintained its high state of readiness, but the need to push a convoy of reinforcements across the autobahn had receded. In addition, everyone recognized that, for all their training and equipment, American personnel were hostages in an international contest of wills. If the Soviets and East Germans decided to attack, the Berlin Brigade could only slow them down. The American soldiers and airmen accepted the risk.

> *"There were ten thousand Americans in Berlin, and we always said that if the Russians wanted to take Berlin, all they had to do was put POW signs around the Wall. . . . Other than the fact we could drive a tank down the road with the American flag on it, we didn't have a chance.*
>
> *". . . I was in the intelligence business. I knew there were twenty Russian divisions in East Germany. We didn't have a chance. But no, I didn't feel under siege."*
>
> *Captain James Graham, U.S. Air Force, Berlin, 1969–1973*

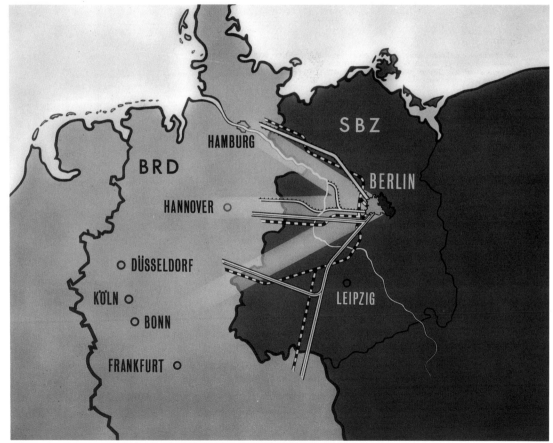

This West German map uses abbreviations that reflect the attitudes of the 1960s. BRD is the German abbreviation for the Federal Republic of Germany, SBZ for the Soviet Zone of Occupation. Access to Berlin across East Germany was restricted to designated air, rail, and highway corridors.

From his station at Tempelhof, an airman monitors air traffic in the corridors to Berlin.

The Wall as Education

President Kennedy's visit to Berlin underscored how the Wall symbolized the differences between two systems. The prominent radio and television journalist Edward R. Murrow, who served the Kennedy administration as director of the U.S. Information Agency between 1961 and 1964, described the symbolism tellingly:

> *The largest educational machine in the world is in Berlin. It is 27 miles long. It is strung with barbed wire. It teaches lessons in the meaning of democracy and communism, of freedom and tyranny, of humanity and in-humanity. Its name is The Wall.*

The West German government quickly realized the educational value of the Wall and encouraged visitors to West Berlin to see it. Travel bureaus in West Germany began including the Wall in tour bookings to Berlin as soon as the fear of a military clash subsided. By the summer of 1962, it was a regular stop for visitors to West Berlin.

The government of the Federal Republic of Germany subsidized airplane fares to Berlin, keeping the cost within reach of more travelers. It also sponsored tours to Berlin for visiting scholars, journalists, and students, letting them see the Wall first hand.

The government also furnished information, emphasizing the perniciousness of the regime that had resorted to building the Wall. Visitors found wooden viewing platforms along the Wall at opportune points where they could see

"The Wall—we'd read about it, and seen pictures, but to see that ugly thing through the center of the city—and no-man's-land—we hadn't imagined that swath of wasteland right through the middle of the city. That made an impression.

"When you ride along the Wall, you can't see over it, but when you get up on the viewing stand and see nothing—that's what left an impression. To look out and see nothing."

Martin Reuss, American exchange student in Germany, 1965

From viewing stands constructed at the Wall, West Berliners could see friends or relatives in the East.

"It's a Sunday afternoon. We're standing on the [observation] tower. There's a lady, clearly a grandmother, standing there on the tower, tears rolling out of her eyes. Walking along the street, coming toward us, is a younger girl with a baby. She holds the baby up and this is clearly mom on this side, and the daughter is on the east side. They're showing her the grandchild, and, as I recall, [the young woman] slowed down a little bit and then one of the Vopos [Volkspolitzei, East German police] came along and pushed her to get her moving again.

"This was a very common sight at these observation points. Remember, this is less than ten years after that Wall went up, so you've still got families that were separated, that hadn't been able to get together. . . . I felt like crying, too. It was very sad."

Captain James Graham,
U.S. Air Force, Berlin, 1969–1973

125

1945
1946
1947
1948
1949
1950
1951
1952
1953
1954
1955
1956
1957
1958
1959
1960
1961
1962
1963
1964
1965
1966
1967
1968
1969
1970
1971
1972
1973
1974
1975
1976
1977
1978
1979
1980
1981
1982
1983
1984
1985
1986
1987
1988
1989
1990
1991
1992
1993
1994

over into East Berlin. Experiencing the Wall bolstered the perception of Berlin as an outpost of freedom. No amount of data could match seeing the Wall itself.

Change in West German Foreign Policy

The Wall forced West Germans to realize that, unless they came to terms with the Soviet Union, the situation of their compatriots in East Germany would never improve. Neither the barrier dividing Berlin nor the East German state would just go away.

Since the creation of the Federal Republic of Germany, West German foreign policy had subordinated unification to forging a solid alliance with the United States and Western Europe. As a cornerstone of foreign policy, West German governments had refused to recognize either the loss of German territory resulting from the German defeat in the war or the legitimacy of the East German state. The international situation, and the Berlin Wall, made it clear by the early 1960s that a policy of denial had led to a dead end.

Changes in West German foreign policy proceeded only grudgingly. Tentative efforts towards a new policy suffered a major disruption when the Soviet Union invaded Czechoslovakia in August 1968 to suppress that country's modest program of reform.

Federal elections of September 1969 accelerated the pace of change in West German foreign policy. The Social Democratic Party took control of the cabinet, and party leader Willy Brandt,

mayor of Berlin when the Wall went up in 1961, became chancellor. He firmly believed that improvements would come only through a foreign policy of opening to the Soviet Union and Eastern Europe. Theoretically, West Germans might assert a right to territories now held by the Soviet Union, Poland, and Czechoslovakia. Practically, Brandt contended that it was time to emphasize living people rather than outworn legal claims to land lost because of the German defeat in the war.

With great energy, Brandt pursued talks with the Soviet Union and Poland. At the same time, he explored contacts with a reluctant East German government. He encouraged the three western powers with troops in Berlin to negotiate with the Soviet Union concerning the city's status.

Brandt's actions quickly brought results. In August 1970, he signed the Treaty of Moscow with the Soviet Union and before the end of the year the Treaty of Warsaw with Poland. In the treaties Brandt renounced the use of force to modify any frontiers in Eastern Europe and recognized the Polish and Russian borders as "inviolable." He also suggested a willingness to come to terms with the East German state so long as he could preserve the right to reunification through a free vote of the German people.

Europe was divided into East and West, with Berlin a divided city located in the East.

Growing prosperity in West Berlin was evident to all who visited the Kurfürstendamm, the major shopping street.

126

1945
1946
1947
1948
1949
1950
1951
1952
1953
1954
1955
1956
1957
1958
1959
1960
1961
1962
1963
1964
1965
1966
1967
1968
1969
1970
1971
1972
1973
1974
1975
1976
1977
1978
1979
1980
1981
1982
1983
1984
1985
1986
1987
1988
1989
1990
1991
1992
1993
1994

Quadripartite Agreement

Brandt carefully informed his western allies and partners in NATO as he carried the negotiations forward. He also delayed West German ratification of the Moscow Treaty until the four powers could reach an agreement on the status of Berlin. By linking reconciliation with the Soviet Union to settling the status of Berlin, Brandt pushed the four powers to compromise on the divided city.

In early September 1971, the four powers signed an accord on Berlin. The parties excluded any clear definition of Berlin in the text of the agreements to avoid the controversial distinction between East and West Berlin. Instead, the text affirmed the individual and joint responsibilities of all four powers "in the relevant area." The Soviet Union recognized the western powers' rights of access to the city. The western powers affirmed the exclusion of the western sectors of Berlin from the territories of the Federal Republic. The accord did not mention East or West Berlin at all, and the western powers maintained their claim to four-power rights throughout the city.

The Soviet Union abandoned its contention that West Berlin lay on East German territory and conceded to the West German government the right to represent West Berlin diplomatically. The Soviets extended to West Berliners the right to travel to East Germany and East Berlin, prohibited since the construction of the Wall. They also promised to end the slowdown of traffic between West Germany and Berlin. All four powers also renounced the use of force in Berlin and committed themselves to resolve through negotiations all future problems concerning the city.

The quadripartite accord did not really solve the Berlin problem. The agreements did defuse Berlin as a point of international tension. They laid out terms that all parties could accept as a tolerable environment for everyday life. The accords provided the framework for solving such practical matters as the status of Steinstücken. Negotiations secured the right of access to West Berlin for Steinstücken's residents. With that the Berlin Brigade withdrew its three-man military police detachment stationed in the town since 1961.

In December 1971, Brandt received the Nobel Peace Prize for his success in reducing the tensions of the Cold War. Through the spring of 1972, his *Ostpolitik* (opening to the East) knit together the skeins of a comprehensive settlement. The last element was an accord between the two German states that included the specific arrangements concerning Berlin. This German-German treaty opened the way for the ratification by the West German parliament of the Moscow and Warsaw treaties. The implementation of the four-power accord on Berlin followed shortly thereafter.

> "I went down to the John F. Kennedy Platz and listened to the announcement of the four-power quadripartite agreement, because I wanted to be there that day. I was one of thousands of people in a massive crowd as they made that announcement. It was an exciting time. I had watched tensions lessen."
>
> *Captain James Graham,*
> *U.S. Air Force, Berlin, 1969–1973*

Beginning in 1962, Checkpoint Charlie
at Friedrichstrasse became an allied
control point. British, French, and
American military police monitored
the crossing from a guardhouse.

1945
1946
1947
1948
1949
1950
1951
1952
1953
1954
1955
1956
1957
1958
1959
1960
1961
1962
1963
1964
1965
1966
1967
1968
1969
1970
1971
1972
1973
1974
1975
1976
1977
1978
1979
1980
1981
1982
1983
1984
1985
1986
1987
1988
1989
1990
1991
1992
1993
1994

American Soldiers and the Changing Times

Throughout the period in which Chancellor Brandt pursued his Ostpolitik, the United States faced the divisive tensions generated by its involvement in Vietnam. The U.S. military had to deal with the government's attention to the war in Vietnam on several levels.

By 1968, the needs of the military in Southeast Asia shortened tours in Berlin, and the brigade experienced a decline from its maximum strength. The brigade set up specialized training for personnel scheduled to transfer to Vietnam, drawing on the experience of its combat veterans. By 1971, the brigade had recovered from personnel shortages to reach 101 percent of its authorized strength.

The Berlin Command had to deal with social issues exacerbated by the experience of Vietnam and the crisis in morale that it caused. The command instituted programs to address drug and alcohol abuse, although comparative statistics suggest that such abuse was less prevalent in Berlin than in other locations.

Reflecting one of the major revolutions in American society during the 1960s, the Berlin Command developed a new sensitivity to the issues of racial and ethnic minorities. The command appointed race relations personnel and sent them to the first course of the Defense Race Relations Institute. Beginning in 1972, the Berlin Brigade instituted a series of race relations seminars for military and civilian personnel. In November 1973, the Berlin Brigade hosted a three-day *Ethnic Expo 73*, that invited the entire community to learn from the diversity of cultural heritages that make up the American mosaic.

Throughout the turbulence that the American involvement in Vietnam brought and the hostility that it provoked, the relations between Berliners and American soldiers in their midst remained remarkably cordial. By 1967, every municipal district in the American sector celebrated a German-American friendship day or sponsored a Fourth of July parade. American soldiers and their families mingled with West Berliners at Volksfests, sharing beer, sausages, songs, and fellowship.

"The day we arrived [August 1969] was the beginning of the German-American Volksfest, held by the Berlin Brigade every August, a big festival on the other side of the fence from our apartment. Eleven o'clock at night, and out your window is the oompah-pah band and the people drinking beer in a beer tent—it's hard to go to sleep. So we adopted an 'if you can't beat 'em, join 'em' attitude, put our clothes on and went through the fence to sit in the tent and drink beer. We learned German singing and German music and German customs real quick. And we had a good time with it."

Captain James Graham, U.S. Air Force, Berlin, 1969–1973

The Berlin Brigade's German-American Volksfest was held near military housing in the American sector.

American military families in Berlin through the 1960s and 1970s raised their children and sent them to school. The U.S. Army hospital in Berlin continued its long service to the community. The hospital had delivered the first newborn dependent in December 1946, and its maternity service served new mothers with each rotation of troops.

Jennie Graham
in Berlin

The U.S. Army hospital in Berlin served military personnel and their families.

Children born in Berlin to American
military were issued four birth documents,
underscoring the fact that Berlin was not a
part of any nation or state.

The American community entertained West Berliners at open houses on the American compounds, welcoming each year tens of thousands of local citizens who came to look at the military equipment on display. In 1970, Air Force Colonel Gail S. Halvorsen returned to the city as base commander at Tempelhof. West Berliners who as children had picked up the candy dropped by Halvorsen during the airlift enjoyed meeting and thanking him. In 1973, Halvorsen participated in a commemorative celebration of the 25th anniversary of the airlift at the Tempelhof open house which attracted a record crowd of 300,000 visitors.

A scrapbook details the 1973 Tempelhof open house and the 25th anniversary of the airlift.

Col. Gail S. Halvorsen, base commander at Tempelhof from 1970 to 1974, posed with a handkerchief parachute in front of the Airlift Memorial.

Crowds poured through the gates to inspect aircraft on display at Tempelhof.

Tempelhof air base housed Headquarters, U.S. Air Forces in Berlin.

A C-47 plane, veteran of the Berlin airlift, placed on the outline of a C-5 transport on the tarmac at Tempelhof shows the increased capacity of the newer, larger aircraft. U.S. Air Force photographer Helga Mellmann took this photo from a helicopter.

Reduced Tensions

In the years after the quadripartite accord, freedom of movement improved for West Berliners and the risk of war declined, but the Wall remained. Initially, the Wall represented a diplomatic defeat for the United States. It forced West Germany to make changes in its foreign policy as the 1960s progressed. By 1973, the West German government had concluded treaties that confirmed the existing territorial distribution in Eastern Europe. The Brandt government had also learned to speak of two German states in one German nation. The West Germans held tenaciously to the right of the German people to vote at some future date for German unification—one state and one nation—but they had come to terms with existing realities.

For the Soviet Union and East Germany, the Wall still represented an embarrassment. All their sophistry could not justify the need for a wall to keep their population from fleeing. The Wall stopped the migration, but at a moral cost that became increasingly burdensome.

The Cold War did not end with the agreements stemming from West German Ostpolitik. Tensions in Berlin subsided after 1973, but the city remained a center of intrigue and a point of passage for international terrorists moving between the East and West.

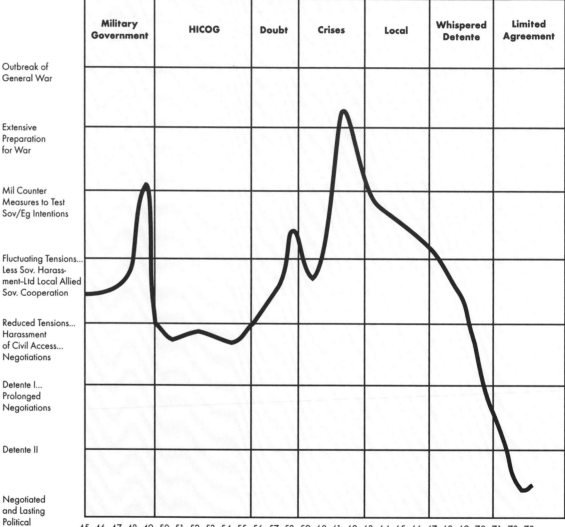

CURVE OF TENSION

A Graphic Representation of Berlin's History, 1945-73

This 1978 graph depicting the rise and fall in perceived tension in Berlin was prepared for a briefing for the U.S. Commander, Berlin.

The first Allied Forces Day Parade was held in April 1964. Although the month and location changed, it became an annual event.

Living with the Wall
1973–1988

The quadripartite agreements and the Ostpolitik of the Brandt government improved the lives of West Berlin's residents. Very quickly, their sense of isolation from the rest of the world diminished.

East-West Contacts

Within two years of the agreements, travel across the autobahn to West Germany increased by two-thirds. West Berliners could now take vacations, even weekend trips, by car. A two-hour drive brought them to West Germany, and many began to make the trip regularly. To speed the handling of peak traffic, the East Germans expanded checkpoints to multiple lanes at their borders. West Germans did not have to get out of their cars. The East Germans rarely searched vehicles. Transport trucks sealed by western customs officers traveled unchallenged across East Germany. The fees collected from the traffic brought the East German economy substantial sums of badly needed hard currency.

Contacts between West and East Berliners, essentially forbidden before the quadripartite accord, increased quickly. In the final six months of 1972, after the accords were implemented in June, over

2 million West Berliners crossed the Wall for visits of one or more days. The next year, the number of visits almost doubled. Phone calls between West and East Berlin were prohibited in 1970. In 1972, West Berliners made 2.9 million calls to East Berlin.

"If you were driving through [East Germany to Berlin], you had to have a certified full tank of gas, you had to sit for a 20- to 30-minute briefing on the route, and you had a route book. It had photographs of the key signs to look for.... It had pages in Russian that said, 'Take me to your leader.' 'I want to see a Russian officer now.' 'Please assist me, my car has broken down.' You know, the key things you'd run into. And then it went into strip maps and then, behind the strip maps, were actual photographs of the highway as you were going to see it."

Tom Starbuck, civilian employee, U.S. Army

Facilities at Checkpoint Alfa on the autobahn heading from Helmstedt into East Germany, shown here in the late 1960s, were expanded after the agreements of 1972.

Brandenburg Gate in 1973

1945
1946
1947
1948
1949
1950
1951
1952
1953
1954
1955
1956
1957
1958
1959
1960
1961
1962
1963
1964
1965
1966
1967
1968
1969
1970
1971
1972
1973
1974
1975
1976
1977
1978
1979
1980
1981
1982
1983
1984
1985
1986
1987
1988
1989
1990
1991
1992
1993
1994

Unlike West Berliners, West Germans could travel to East Germany before the accord, but their travel also increased. Those spending a day or more in the German Democratic Republic numbered 1.2 million in 1971 (before the accord), almost 2.3 million by 1973, and 3.1 million by 1975.

Telephone calls and travel between East and West Germany confirm that contacts between residents of the two states had become more routine by the mid-1970s. In spite of the Wall, life in Berlin also seemed nearly normal. Transit travel from West Berlin *through* East Germany to the Federal Republic seldom involved more than paying a fee.

Still, travel *to* East Germany or East Berlin was not entirely open. It required applications, forms, and the mandatory purchase of East German marks at an exchange rate so unfavorable that it amounted to an admissions fee. The movement of people was also one-way. East Germans could not travel to the West.

Early facilities built at the Checkpoint Bravo border crossing were still in use at the end of the 1950s.

"*[Traveling from West Germany to Berlin] when you got to Checkpoint Bravo, you went upstairs, turned in your little green book, signed in. They had a questionnaire that you filled out about any suspicious activities. If you noticed any military convoys crossing or near the highway, you wrote down the number of vehicles observed, which direction they were headed, any unit markings. We were in the business of intelligence gathering to a limited degree during our crossing.... The whole process took anywhere from three to four hours to make a 180-kilometer drive.*"

Tom Starbuck, civilian employee, U.S. Army

By the late 1960s, the allies had built new facilities at Checkpoint Bravo.

"If it took you too long [to drive across East Germany], we were told the Russians would get upset; they'd think you were spying. If you got there too quick, the American MPs would give you a speeding ticket."

Sergeant Dan Lucas, U.S. Army, Berlin, 1977–1979

A macabre traffic sign reminded travelers bound for Berlin to be cautious and alert.

"You couldn't just go for a drive in the country. It was a big deal to get out of Berlin unless you flew. To drive or take the duty train, you had to get flag orders ... go to Checkpoint Bravo, go to the American MPs, show the flag orders, drive up, talk to the East Germans or Russians—since we were in the military, we'd talk to the Russians. They'd take forever to look over the flag orders, and they'd offer us trinkets— belt buckles, that sort of thing. ... They wanted cash."

Sergeant Dan Lucas, U.S. Army, Berlin, 1977–1979

DO NOT CROSS THE AUTOBAHN

1945
1946
1947
1948
1949
1950
1951
1952
1953
1954
1955
1956
1957
1958
1959
1960
1961
1962
1963
1964
1965
1966
1967
1968
1969
1970
1971
1972
1973
1974
1975
1976
1977
1978
1979
1980
1981
1982
1983
1984
1985
1986
1987
1988
1989
1990
1991
1992
1993
1994

American military personnel still faced all the rigors of travel across East Germany to West Berlin that had existed since the late 1940s. They had to pass checkpoints Alfa and Bravo at both the west and east ends of the autobahn and follow a rigid schedule in transit. For them and their families, travel to West Berlin through East Germany remained time-consuming and unnerving.

Under these conditions, normal was more a perceived than a measurable status. Whereas some West Berliners adapted to the situation, others voiced concern that, with the outside world paying less attention, the city might quietly succumb to Soviet pressures and ultimately fall to communism.

"You had to have flag orders, a paper with the American flag on the top. It was in Russian and English. It was meticulously filled out. One mistake, it's no good. It was two-sided, and the front had to agree with the back. The Soviets would look at front and back to make sure that the numbers matched . . . down to the minutest detail. It had to match your passport. If there was a space between two digits on your passport and they didn't space it on your flag orders, they would reject you. It was nothing more than harassment. Depending on the political climate, they would play with you more or less."

Tom Starbuck, civilian employee, U.S. Army

By the late 1980s, the American flag on travel papers, called flag orders, was printed in color.

Front

Back

ATTENTION!
ALL PASSENGERS WILL CONFIRM RETURN SPACE OR
REQUEST RETURN RESERVATION AT WINDOW #6 IN THE
RTO IMMEDIATELY AFTER DETRAINING. FAILURE TO DO
SO MAY RESULT IN NON-AVAILABILITY OF DESIRED SPACE
ON TRAIN FOR RETURN TRIP

118 072-8

"For the duty train, you had to get flag orders. They'd stop you going into East Germany and leaving East Germany. It gave you a feeling of being closed in."

Sergeant Dan Lucas, U.S. Army, Berlin, 1977–1979

The duty train, available to American military personnel and dependents, made the overnight trip between Berlin and Frankfurt, West Germany.

"[On the duty train] you had to stop at Magdeburg. They had an American officer that had to get off with everybody's passport and these flag orders, [with] a Russian translator, and go into a building. And you'd sit there sometimes an hour or more while they checked every paper. Then they'd come back out and get on the train. Meanwhile, guys are walking on both sides of the train with submachine guns trained on you—very, very intimidating."

Tom Starbuck, civilian employee, U.S. Army

1945
1946
1947
1948
1949
1950
1951
1952
1953
1954
1955
1956
1957
1958
1959
1960
1961
1962
1963
1964
1965
1966
1967
1968
1969
1970
1971
1972
1973
1974
1975
1976
1977
1978
1979
1980
1981
1982
1983
1984
1985
1986
1987
1988
1989
1990
1991
1992
1993
1994

Unchanged Mission

By the mid-1970s, the Cold War no longer focused on Berlin. The Middle East and Africa had supplanted Central Europe as the center of crisis and attention. Nonetheless, the presence of allied troops and the American Berlin Command remained a hedge against East Germany's absorbing West Berlin. The American military mission in Berlin did not change: to protect West Berlin against any possible aggression and to assert American rights under the four-power accords.

The U.S. Commander, Berlin, continued to exercise his multiple authority. As U.S. commandant in Berlin, following directives from the U.S. European Command, he protected the interests of the United States and exercised all the prerogatives associated with four-power rights. As the deputy chief of the U.S. Mission in Berlin, he fulfilled diplomatic responsibilities, answering to the United States Ambassador to the Federal Republic of Germany. As the commander of U.S. Army, Berlin, he exercised direct command authority over Army units in the city and represented the commander in chief, U.S. Army, Europe.

Through the 1970s and 1980s, the U.S. Commander, Berlin, continued his intelligence, political, and public information functions in addition to his duties as a troop commander. All the activities attached to the Berlin Command involved publicly demonstrating American intentions to stay in the city until the four powers found a satisfactory settlement of World War II.

Soldiers monitored traffic at the allied crossing, Checkpoint Charlie, where the small building and informal sign had been replaced.

"East Berlin was really depressing. I went there once or twice, and it was so depressing I couldn't go anymore. The people couldn't have been nicer in the stores, super helpful, very pleased to see us. I bought a couple of records and some other things, but I felt sorry for them. All the buildings were run down. We'd drive by a taxi stand, there'd be 30 people in line, waiting for a taxi. It was very depressing. We'd go into stores—they had a smell about them, real cheap, and very few things in them … not much available compared to West Germany. It was pitiful … buildings bombed out, never rebuilt. A lot of it was still awful."

Sergeant Dan Lucas, U.S. Army, Berlin, 1977–1979

As part of its readiness training in the 1970s, members of the Military Airlift Command practiced for another airlift.

Because tension decreased after the quadripartite accord, the need to maintain the sense of mission among the troops increased. Training continued in the wooded areas of West Berlin, and inter-allied field training continued at the battalion level with British and French units stationed in Berlin. Because training with live ammunition was limited within the city, units from the Berlin Brigade regularly visited training areas in West Germany such as the tank range at Grafenwöhr. In the spring of 1975, the Army opened a new urban combat training facility at Parks Range on property formerly owned by the German railway system. This mock village updated the training facilities that the troops had used since the 1950s. It became known as "Doughboy City."

The Army added adventure training to its program in the early 1970s. It did not substitute for standard training but encouraged and rewarded leadership, fostered camaraderie, and provided exciting excursions. From 1973 to 1974, units of the Berlin Brigade participated in mountain training in Italy, France, and Scotland; ski training in southern Germany; kayaking across the English Channel; and reenacting the June 6, 1944, landing in France by scaling the cliffs behind the Normandy beaches.

Members of the 4th Battalion, 6th Infantry, devised a novel way to emphasize their presence in the city when, in January 1975, they staged the first Berlin Wall marathon. The U.S. Commander, Berlin, the commander of the Berlin Brigade, and members of the general staff participated in the event. Runners moving in

The soldiers trained for urban warfare in Doughboy City.

BERLIN MILITARY TRAINING AREAS

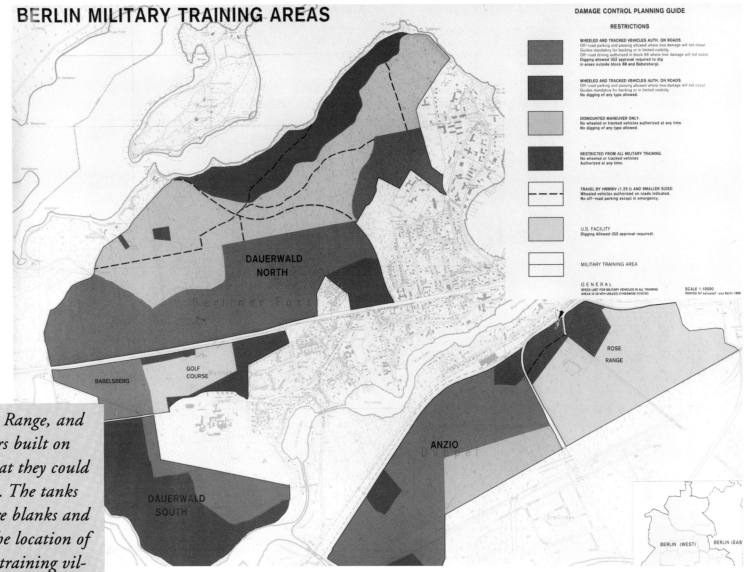

"The Wall adjoined Parks Range, and the Soviets had large towers built on their side of the Wall so that they could observe all of our training. The tanks would go out there and fire blanks and play around. That's also the location of Doughboy City, the mock training village. They would watch our infantry tactics and take photographs, and we'd wave to them. It was quite unique."

Tom Starbuck, civilian employee, U.S. Army

relays covered the entire 100-mile circumference of the Wall, an inescapable reminder of why the American troops were there. The marathon became an annual event.

In the mid-1970s, air traffic patterns changed in Berlin. In the early 1960s, commercial jet airliners began landing at Tegel in the French sector because it had longer runways. Although Tempelhof handled both commercial and military traffic, including jet aircraft, buildings surrounding the airfield limited the length of its runways. The West Berlin government had developed plans in 1966 to expand Tegel, and by 1975 the expansion was completed. On September 1 all commercial traffic shifted from Tempelhof to the Tegel air terminal. Tempelhof continued as a military airfield, which the Air Force kept equipped with the latest electronic facilities.

Since 1963, Tempelhof had attracted skyjackers and refugees seeking to escape by air from Eastern Europe. It remained their destination of choice even after its conversion to exclusively military use. Flights carrying escapees continued to land at Tempelhof into the 1980s.

A new long-range radar tower to aid navigation was installed at Tempelhof Central Airport (TCA) in 1982.

Some people sought freedom in the West by flying stolen or hijacked airplanes into Berlin. This YAK-12A aircraft, with three Poles seeking political asylum, landed at Tempelhof Central Airport June 12, 1982.

Hijackings to West Berlin, 1963–1983

DATE	TYPE OF INCIDENT	AIRCRAFT	PEOPLE INVOLVED
10 Jul 63	Polish Air Force Officer Stole Plane	TS-8 Bies Trainer	4 Poles: Man, Wife, Children
19 Oct 69	Hijacked to Tegel Warsaw - Schonefeld	AN-24	2 East Berliners
30 Aug 78	Hijacked to TCA Gdansk - Schonefeld	TU-134	1 East German
4 Dec 80	Hijacked to TCA Zielona Gora - Warsaw	AN-24	1 Pole
21 Jul 81	Hijacked to TCA Katowice - Gdansk	AN-24	1 Pole
22 Aug 81	Hijacked to TCA Wroclaw - Warsaw	AN-24	1 Pole
18 Sep 81	Hijacked to TCA Katowice - Warsaw	AN-24	12 Polish Students
12 Feb 82	Unscheduled Landing TCA Warsaw-Wroclaw	AN-24	2 Poles with Families
30 Apr 82	Hijacked to TCA Wroclaw - Warsaw	AN-24	8 Poles
12 Jun 82	Aircraft stolen from Flying Club	YAK-12A	3 Poles
22 Nov 82	Hijacked to TCA Wroclaw - Warsaw	AN-24	1 Polish Military Man
26 Jan 83	Unscheduled Landing TCA	YAK-12A	3 Poles
17 Sep 83	Unscheduled Landing TCA	AN-12	9 Poles
25 Oct 83	Unscheduled Landing TCA	YAK-12	4 Poles

Naming Headquarters

The death of Lucius D. Clay in April 1978 saddened Berliners. They believed that he had helped secure the American commitment to preserve West Berlin's freedom by his leadership during the Berlin airlift. His service in 1961 and 1962 had reconfirmed their bond with him. After the Soviet blockade ended in 1949, the city government of West Berlin had changed the name of Kronprinzenallee, on which the U.S. Headquarters was situated, to Clayallee.

Gen. Lucius D. Clay, retiring military governor of Germany, on a visit to the Pentagon in May 1949.

The Army had named facilities in the American sector after deceased servicemen; as long as Clay lived, military protocol dictated that his name not be used. The Army left unnamed the headquarters from which Clay had governed Germany for nearly four years. On May 12, 1979, the 30th anniversary of the lifting of the Soviet blockade of Berlin, the Army held a ceremony at the Clayallee compound. With General Clay's widow, two of his sons, and dignitaries from the West Berlin government present, the compound officially became General Lucius D. Clay Headquarters.

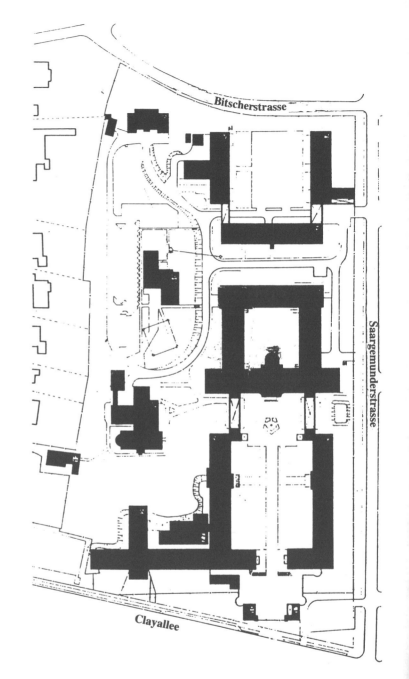

Clay Headquarters is a 19-acre compound occupied by ten major buildings which housed the offices of the Commandant, U.S. Army, Berlin; the Commander, Berlin Brigade; the U.S. Minister, Department of State; and their administrative staffs.

1945
1946
1947
1948
1949
1950
1951
1952
1953
1954
1955
1956
1957
1958
1959
1960
1961
1962
1963
1964
1965
1966
1967
1968
1969
1970
1971
1972
1973
1974
1975
1976
1977
1978
1979
1980
1981
1982
1983
1984
1985
1986
1987
1988
1989
1990
1991
1992
1993
1994

Persistent Uncertainties

Tension diminished for most West Berliners after the quadripartite agreements, and recognition of the eastern German Democratic Republic followed. In September 1973, both German states joined the United Nations. In 1974, the United States prepared to open an embassy in East Berlin. Still, tension did not disappear.

Differences in interpreting the four-power accords provoked open clashes of interest. Throughout 1973 and the first half of 1974, the Soviet Union objected to plans by the Federal Republic to establish in Berlin an office of the German (Federal) Environment Agency. When the West German government finally opened the office in the summer of 1974, East German and Soviet officials began a series of harassing actions affecting land transportation to and from Berlin. After several days of harassment, the U.S. Department of State announced a postponement of recognition of the German Democratic Republic until the diplomatic atmosphere improved. The harassment stopped, and in September 1974, the United States opened its embassy in East Berlin.

The temporary disruption of overland access to and from Berlin showed that the cordial cooperation following the accords implemented in 1972 could be disrupted at any moment. Tension never reached the levels of the early 1960s, but neither did relations proceed as smoothly as in the months immediately following the quadripartite agreement.

Threats to the allied or American position came indirectly as well as directly. In the mid-1970s, authorities uncovered over 1,000 agents operating covertly against American interests in West Germany. The incidence of terrorism also increased in West Germany. In 1977, a terrorist group, the Red Army Faction, carried out a series of bombings, abductions, and assassinations, including the execution of two West German business leaders and a public prosecutor.

Counterterrorism and espionage played a part in the U.S. military mission in Berlin. By the 1970s, the Berlin Command operated sophisticated electronic listening stations on the Teufelsberg and at Marienfelde to monitor message traffic in East Germany. Electronic eavesdropping was only a part of the command's intelligence gathering.

The U.S. Air Force, 6912th Security Squadron, based at Tempelhof, manned the facility at Marienfelde.

Teufelsberg, a mountain of rubble and the highest point in Berlin, was the location of a voice and signal intercept site used by the U.S. Army, U.S. Air Force, and the British Air Force.

In a 1979 postcard from Berlin, the military facility at Teufelsberg looms over pleasure boats on the Teufelsee.

"Several times when we were out on the town, we were approached by people who were very suspect—on one occasion a Russian and a Polish fellow that seemed to have a lot of knowledge about American military things. That was kind of weird. They [the Army] showed us training films and then to have it actually happen was disquieting. They were feeling us out, to see if they could find out a way to get us to provide some information."

Sergeant Dan Lucas, U.S. Army, Berlin, 1977–1979

1945
1946
1947
1948
1949
1950
1951
1952
1953
1954
1955
1956
1957
1958
1959
1960
1961
1962
1963
1964
1965
1966
1967
1968
1969
1970
1971
1972
1973
1974
1975
1976
1977
1978
1979
1980
1981
1982
1983
1984
1985
1986
1987
1988
1989
1990
1991
1992
1993
1994

The four occupying powers had engaged in military intelligence gathering since they arrived in Berlin. In 1947, they had agreed to accredit liaison missions to operate in one another's zones of occupation and to observe military activities. The Soviet Union operated military liaison missions in all three western zones, with one team near Frankfurt in the American zone. The American counterpart, the U.S. Military Liaison Mission to the Commander in Chief, Soviet Western Group of Forces (USMLM), operated from a 4.5-acre estate near Potsdam in the Soviet zone. The grounds included a substantial villa and four additional buildings.

The U.S. Military Liaison Mission had 14 positions, filled on a rotating basis. Members of the team lived in West Berlin but traveled throughout East Germany from their base in Potsdam. Their mission was to assert the American right to free movement in the zone and to gather intelligence information. The Soviet Union barred access to certain areas, often the ones the Americans most wanted to see. Members of the mission knew that their assignment involved great danger. They expected harassment from Soviet guards. Through the years, team members reported incidents in which they encountered harassment, beatings, and hostile fire. In 1984, a member of the French liaison mission died when an East German Army truck rammed his vehicle head-on.

Deutsche Demokratische Republik

Potsdam

The headquarters of the U.S. Military Liaison Mission was in Potsdam, just outside Berlin.

"A colleague of mine had gone out and seen a military train loaded with missile equipment, had followed in his car and attempted to photograph the missile equipment. And they shot at his car, hit it, knocked out his windows, his tires, and he was left immobile and then was arrested by East German and then Soviet authorities. . . . This happened with a fair amount of frequency . . . it was not unusual for this type of thing to happen."

Lynn Hansen, U.S. Air Force officer, Berlin, 1960–1963, 1971–1975

License plate from the Military Liaison Mission.
The designation in Russian reads "American Military
Mission to the Group of Soviet Forces Germany."

License plate for a vehicle with the Soviet
Military Mission based in Frankfurt,
West Germany.

"The Soviet Union and the Soviet Army were our enemy. It was very strongly felt, and each time we crossed the bridge from West Berlin into East Germany, we entered a hostile territory where we were out there to do whatever we could that would enhance our chances in terms of conflict. We were to collect whatever intelligence we could, and measure the risk—the bodily risk toward ourselves—which could be considerable.... There were 14 Americans, 32 British and 18 French, if my memory serves me correctly, who had this opportunity to go out into East Germany every day and to observe what the Soviet Army was doing."

Lynn Hansen, U.S. Air Force officer, Berlin, 1960–1963, 1971–1975

Major Nicholson's Death

On Sunday, March 24, 1985, a member of the American liaison unit, Major Arthur D. Nicholson, Jr., left the mission house near Potsdam with his driver, Sergeant Jessie Schatz, on a routine drive. They drove north to the vicinity of Ludwigslust, the location of a Soviet tank regiment. Shortly before 4:00 that afternoon, Nicholson left the car to walk toward a Soviet tank shed to take pictures through a window. A Soviet guard appeared and fired three rounds from his AK-47 rifle, one of which hit Major Nicholson. When Schatz tried to help Nicholson, Soviet guards stopped him. An hour elapsed before a Soviet medic arrived. By that time, Nicholson was dead. The next day, an East German ambulance delivered Nicholson's body to a U.S. Army honor guard at the Glienecke Bridge between East and West Berlin in the American sector.

The United States government protested the shooting, asserting that Nicholson had followed all the established procedures governing the work of the Military Liaison Mission. He was in uniform, his vehicle was clearly marked, and he was in an unrestricted area. The Soviets claimed that he had been in a restricted area, had failed to respond to shouted warnings in Russian and German, had tried to flee, and had not stopped even when the Soviet guard fired a warning shot. After several weeks, the Soviets apologized for the shooting, but they continued to deny responsibility.

Nicholson was the only fatality suffered by the U.S. Military Liaison Mission. The diplomatic treatment of the murder illustrates the extent to which tensions surrounding Berlin and the German problem had abated since the early 1960s. On Saturday, April 6, as Nicholson was buried in Arlington National Cemetery, the Soviet ambassador met with the American secretary of state. They agreed that the commander in chief of the Soviet forces in East Germany and the commander in chief of the U.S. Army, Europe, should meet to develop procedures to avoid such violent episodes in the future. A senior American official in Washington remarked: "We think the Soviet response is something we can build on."

At an earlier time, an incident such as the shooting of Major Nicholson might have escalated to a more dangerous level. All sides, however, had scaled down their concerns over the German question. In addition, the episode occurred shortly after Mikhail Gorbachev assumed power in the Soviet Union. The United States, eager to establish good relations with the new Soviet leader, handled the shooting as an aberration rather than as a sign of Soviet aggression. The death of Major Nicholson was a personal tragedy, but not an international incident.

Nonetheless, the shooting by a Soviet soldier of an American soldier executing a legitimate mission underscored the dangers inherent in military service in Germany and Berlin. The division of the city and the nation remained real and exploitable. The presence of allied forces continued to be necessary, and it also made them a target for those intent on undermining the prevailing stability.

Maj. Arthur D. Nicholson, Jr.

Honor guard escorted the flag-draped casket of Maj. Arthur D. Nicholson, Jr., to Washington, D.C.

The library for the American military community in Berlin was dedicated and named the Arthur D. Nicholson, Jr., Library.

The Terror Bombing of La Belle Club

Nicholson died because of a direct confrontation with the Soviet Army stationed in East Germany. Two other American soldiers died a year later as the result of a terrorist attack.

In the very early morning of April 5, 1986, a bomb blast destroyed La Belle Club, a discothèque in Berlin's Friedenau neighborhood. About 500 people, many of them American soldiers, were in the building as its stucco walls buckled and its floor collapsed into what the club's disc jockey called a "picture of horror." One American soldier and a 28-year-old Turkish woman were killed in the blast. The explosion wounded nearly 230 people who were taken to nearby Auguste-Viktoria Hospital and to the U.S. Army hospital in Berlin. A second soldier died later of injuries suffered in the blast.

The disco bombing was one incident in a series of attacks against American military personnel. In 1985, terrorists had targeted Americans at restaurants in Athens and Madrid, at a military shopping center in Frankfurt, and at the Rhein-Main air base. Authorities cited 12 major attacks that year on American and allied installations and dozens of lesser incidents. Radical European groups claimed responsibility for several of the attacks. American intelligence information from its electronic listening posts tied the Libyan embassy in East Berlin to the disco bombing.

The evidence persuaded President Ronald Reagan to launch a retaliatory air strike against Libya. On April 14, 1986, despite disapproval from nearly all of its European allies, the United States attacked Libya, citing "self defense," to deter Libya from future terrorist action. Eighteen F-111 bombers and 15 A-6 and A-7 attack jets raided five Libyan targets associated with the country's "terrorist infrastructure," including command and control centers and communications, training, and logistics facilities. The American aircraft also targeted the headquarters of Libya's chief of state, Colonel Muammar el-Qaddafi, in Tripoli.

In speaking about the attack, President Reagan claimed, "the evidence is now conclusive that the terrorist bombing of La Belle Club was planned and executed under the direct orders of the Libyan regime." East Germany was quick to condemn the attack on its ally. East German leader, Erich Honecker, denounced the "barbaric bombardment of peaceful Libyan cities" and denied that the Libyan embassy had played a part in the disco bombing. Later evidence revealed not only that the Libyan embassy had been directly involved but that the East German secret police had known of the plans for the bombing of La Belle Club.

Libya claimed 37 people died in the raids, including Qaddafi's adopted infant daughter. The Soviet Union canceled a meeting between Foreign Minister Edward A. Shevardnadze and Secretary of State George P. Shultz, which was to lay the groundwork for a later summit.

The bombing of La Belle Club happened in Berlin, but it did not create a Berlin crisis. The target was the American military establishment, and, because the terrorists operated with the covert aid of the East German secret police, Berlin was simply a convenient location for the attack.

West Berlin police sort through the rubble after the bomb exploded at La Belle Club in the early morning hours of April 5, 1986. Of the 300 people in the club, 2 were killed and 260 injured, including 80 American soldiers.

This poster displayed in American military facilities warned soldiers and employees about potential spies among them.

YOUR BUSINESS... IS THEIR BUSINESS

USCOB POSTER 380-2

The shooting of Major Nicholson and the death of the two servicemen at La Belle Club illustrate the persistent danger faced by the American troops in Berlin even as relations between the United States and the Soviet Union improved. The underlying problems of a divided Germany and an isolated Berlin remained unsolved. The quadripartite accord had alleviated pressures on West Berlin. Nonetheless, the city remained like a hothouse, artificially supported by subsidies from the Federal Republic of Germany and guaranteed by an American military commitment to protect the city's freedom. It was a livable situation, but not self-sustaining.

Gorbachev, Perestroika, and East Germany

The succession of Mikhail S. Gorbachev to the leadership of the Soviet Union in March 1985 did not immediately signal a change in Soviet policy. Yet, one month later, he announced a unilateral moratorium on deployment of new intermediate-range nuclear missiles, and three months after that, he urged reforms of the Soviet economy. In October, a scant half-year after his appointment, he presented a program to initiate economic and political reforms throughout the Soviet system.

Gorbachev called for *perestroika,* a radical restructuring of communist government in a democratic direction, and *glasnost,* or greater freedom of expression. His initiatives toward reform had far-reaching implications for the communist system, both in the Soviet Union and in the East European satellite states.

By 1984, the first, informal memorial for Peter Fechter had been replaced by a larger, more permanent one. Protesters painted graffiti on the Wall behind it.

Through the 1980s East Germans kept the no-man's strip surrounding West Berlin clear, well-lighted, and guarded, making escape unlikely.

1945
1946
1947
1948
1949
1950
1951
1952
1953
1954
1955
1956
1957
1958
1959
1960
1961
1962
1963
1964
1965
1966
1967
1968
1969
1970
1971
1972
1973
1974
1975
1976
1977
1978
1979
1980
1981
1982
1983
1984
1985
1986
1987
1988
1989
1990
1991
1992
1993
1994

No one could measure their significance at the outset, nor be sure that Gorbachev would survive as the country's leader long enough for them to have an impact.

Simultaneously with his calls for internal reform, Gorbachev engaged the United States in a dialogue that led to a disarmament agreement: the Intermediate-range Nuclear Forces (INF) Treaty. Signed by President Ronald Reagan and Gorbachev in Washington on December 8, 1987, the agreement provided for the removal and destruction of 2,611 Soviet and American nuclear missiles, with inspections for verification.

The implications of a Soviet-American understanding, however limited, and Gorbachev's repeated calls for reforms of the communist system made the East German regime of Erich Honecker uneasy. The leaders of East Germany at first tried to ignore Gorbachev's remarks. East Germany's controlled press omitted mention of his most pointed criticisms of past communist practices.

By 1987, as Gorbachev's calls for reform became more insistent, East German leaders began publicly to dismiss them with scorn. East Germany, they contended, had surpassed the Soviet Union in the realization of socialism and therefore did not need the same reforms. Finally, they resorted to suppressing circulation of Soviet publications in the German Democratic Republic because they feared that the contents would subvert their control.

In spite of state repression, a dissident movement had been growing in East Germany since the mid-1970s, and Gorbachev's calls for change emboldened the appeals for reforms within the German Democratic Republic. During 1988, the fervor for reform intensified throughout Eastern Europe. Still, neither the most optimistic dissidents in the East nor the most hopeful officials in the West could foresee the changes that would take place in 1989 and 1990.

Even flower boxes could not obscure the ugly reminders of the East-West separation, such as the wooden barrier blocking the balcony and the bricked-up window in this apartment building adjacent to the Wall in East Berlin.

"[For the 25th anniversary of the Wall] they had special programs on TV and radio. People were interviewed. . . . An older woman, I still hear her, she said, 'Oh, I got used to it. I look at the Wall'—because where she lived she had to look at the Wall—'I have all my flowers on the balcony and I like it. It's so quiet.' My aunt was enraged. She said, 'How can people get used to it?' But they did. It wasn't, of course, the majority. But this was a kind of mentality."

Renate Semler, Berliner

Unification and Withdrawal 1989–1994

The East German regime successfully contained its population's desire for change by building the Berlin Wall which closed all avenues of escape. Knowing that they could not leave, the citizens of the German Democratic Republic grudgingly adjusted to the communist system, and the East German state achieved an aura of stability. In 1989, after 28 years, that stability collapsed suddenly and unexpectedly.

Growing Public Discontent

Gorbachev's promotion of perestroika and glasnost encouraged protesters in East Germany to voice their dissent. At an annual celebration of German communist heroes in January 1989, critics of the government unfurled banners demanding freedom of expression and opposing the regime's oppressive rule. In May, observers dedicated to reforming the system appeared at polling places during local elections to monitor the vote. When the government announced results, always nearly unanimous in East German elections, the dissidents accused the communist officials of

fraud for underreporting the opposition vote and even began legal action. In both cases, the regime arrested the protesters and meted out long prison sentences and exile.

French Sector

WEST BERLIN

British Sector

EAST BERLIN

Soviet Sector

Checkpoint Charlie

American Sector

"People paid, of course, lip service and said, 'Yes. The Wall has to come down.' And everybody wanted it, but nobody foresaw that. I always gave the answer when I was asked by American guests here. I said, 'No. I won't see that in my lifetime. Sometime it will, because it's unnatural.' But I said, 'I won't see it.' I think this was the general statement. Even politicians."

Renate Semler, Berliner

Brandenburg Gate in 1987

1945
1946
1947
1948
1949
1950
1951
1952
1953
1954
1955
1956
1957
1958
1959
1960
1961
1962
1963
1964
1965
1966
1967
1968
1969
1970
1971
1972
1973
1974
1975
1976
1977
1978
1979
1980
1981
1982
1983
1984
1985
1986
1987
1988
1989
1990
1991
1992
1993
1994

No one supposed at the time that these modest protests threatened the East German state. The incidents might have passed unremembered, as had many others, if Hungary, for three decades the most progressive of the Eastern European states, had not moved ahead on its own path to perestroika. The Hungarian government announced its intent to open its borders with Austria, and on May 2, 1989, Hungarian officials began dismantling all barbed wire fences and other barriers between their country and the Austrian Republic.

With Hungary suddenly allowing unhindered access to Austria and the West, East Germans realized they could use traditional vacation travel to circumvent their government's restrictions on emigration. Tens of thousands of East Germans already held valid travel documents for summer trips to Hungary, and by late August, more than 2,000 had successfully fled to West Germany through Hungary and Austria. When Hungarian border guards tried to turn some of the East Germans back, many used unauthorized paths through the open border.

On September 10, the Hungarian government announced that its border guards would no longer honor their prior agreement to stop emigration by East Germans. Within three days, 15,000 East Germans took advantage of the new policy and fled to the West. Hundreds of others, fearing that the East German government would cut off the Hungarian route, sought asylum in the West German embassies in Poland and Czechoslovakia.

The fears that East Germans harbored proved justified. To stop the exodus, the East German regime cut off all travel to Poland and Czechoslovakia early in October. The measure only increased the internal pressures on the government. Domestic demonstrations for reform became more significant.

Peaceful Dissent

In Leipzig, East Germans had held meetings in local churches for several years to pray for peace. In September 1989, the Monday evening prayer meetings took a new form when those gathering for prayer moved out of the churches to conduct peaceful marches through the streets. The police had habitually harassed and occasionally beaten marchers. Nonetheless, participation in the marches grew week by week throughout September. The march of October 2, 1989, attracted 15,000 participants.

The borders of countries in the Warsaw Pact were tightly controlled and passage among them required travel documents. When Hungary opened its borders with Austria on May 2, 1989, East Germans with travel documents to Hungary could pass through Czechoslovakia, Hungary, and Austria to the West.

——— Controlled borders   •••••••••• Border opened May 2, 1989   ▨ Warsaw Pact countries

While East Germans protested and sought to escape through the open Hungarian border, the Wall remained a barrier in Berlin.

167

1945
1946
1947
1948
1949
1950
1951
1952
1953
1954
1955
1956
1957
1958
1959
1960
1961
1962
1963
1964
1965
1966
1967
1968
1969
1970
1971
1972
1973
1974
1975
1976
1977
1978
1979
1980
1981
1982
1983
1984
1985
1986
1987
1988
1989
1990
1991
1992
1993
1994

During the week after the October 2 demonstration, the East German government moved units of the People's Police, supported by the army, into Leipzig. Demonstrators were undeterred by the show of force. A crowd of 70,000 people marched on October 9. To the surprise and relief of the demonstrators, the police and military units did not use the force at their disposal, and the march proceeded peacefully.

The peaceful march in Leipzig on October 9 marked a turning point. A week later, 100,000 people demonstrated. The next day, October 17, the East German party council forced Erich Honecker to resign as party secretary. Having refrained from violence against the demonstrators on October 9, the government now faced crowds that it could not control. On October 23, the crowd in Leipzig swelled to 300,000.

The new East German government arranged for a limited reopening of the border with Czechoslovakia, to take effect on November 3. The hemorrhage began again: within a week, 48,000 East Germans had emigrated through Czechoslovakia and on to West Germany. Dissidents were not mollified. On November 4, 500,000 people gathered in East Berlin to demand reforms of the communist system. On November 6, another 500,000 demonstrated in Leipzig. On November 7, the members of the government cabinet resigned.

The Final Abdication

On November 9, after an all-day meeting of the party council, East Berlin's party boss reported to the public and the press. At the end of a long description of the deliberations, he mentioned a new law governing travel. He seemed to indicate that anyone who wished to go to West Germany, for whatever reasons, could get an exit visa at the border. Radio reports and television excerpts from the official's remarks led crowds of East Berliners to checkpoints at the Wall to test the new regulations.

Astonished border guards, who had received no specific instructions, bowed to the eager crowds and opened the passages to West Berlin. The crowds grew so large that the guards could not process all of their identity papers, so people simply walked through checkpoints. On the western side, they found a huge street party of welcoming West Berliners, a scene of jubilation televised around the world. Berliners celebrated their new freedom by dancing on top of the Wall. Whether by plan or through ineptitude, the Wall had been irrevocably breached.

A lone East German soldier walks atop the Wall, watching the excited crowds on both sides, November 9, 1989.

> "I was in Berlin in October of 1989, spent four or five days in the city. Never, ever, during that time went down and saw the Wall. And a month later it fell. . . . We spent the entire time visiting friends, not even thinking that—I mean, the Hungarian refugees were coming in, but we never, never thought that the Wall was going to fall the way it did. . . . I was amazed."
>
> Colonel James Graham, U.S. Air Force, retired

Towards German Unity

When East Germans passed through the Wall on the night of November 9, a new future opened for all Germans. Berlin ceased to be a divided city. The Wall became an artifact, not a barrier. New passages were punched through the Wall, both officially and spontaneously. Soon, people began chipping out and collecting pieces of the Wall, first as souvenir hunters, then as entrepreneurs. Ironically this symbol of communism quickly became a capitalistic commodity.

East German police and West German citizens watch as workmen dismantle sections of the Wall at Potsdamer Platz from November 14 to 21, 1989, before the official opening of the Brandenburg Gate, December 22, 1989.

Crowds greet East Germans arriving at Checkpoint Charlie in their Trabants, plastic and fiberboard vehicles equipped with two-cylinder motorcycle engines. From November 14 to 21, 1989, East Germans took advantage of relaxed travel restrictions.

Two East German soldiers watch a section of the Wall as it is lifted, November 1989.

People stroll through the new opening of the Wall at Potsdamer Platz, November 1989.

1945
1946
1947
1948
1949
1950
1951
1952
1953
1954
1955
1956
1957
1958
1959
1960
1961
1962
1963
1964
1965
1966
1967
1968
1969
1970
1971
1972
1973
1974
1975
1976
1977
1978
1979
1980
1981
1982
1983
1984
1985
1986
1987
1988
1989
1990
1991
1992
1993
1994

In the first four days after the Wall opened, 4.3 million East Germans visited West Berlin. Most of them returned to their homes in the East, but they had a heightened expectation of change. The leadership of the communist-dominated Social Unity Party had thoroughly discredited itself. By the end of December 1989, the party politburo and central committee had been dissolved.

A new government scheduled East Germany's first free elections for March 18, 1990. As the elections approached, the economic collapse of the East German state became increasingly evident. East Germans continued to leave the country at the rate of 2,000 a day. The East German state could neither control its own economy nor command the allegiance of its own citizens. Popular pressure for unification with West Germany became so strong that it was impossible for the leaders in either state to ignore.

The elections of March 18, 1990, resulted in a resounding victory for the conservative Christian Democratic Union and its supporters, and the movement toward unification accelerated. In mid-May the new East German government signed an agreement to enter an economic union with the Federal Republic of Germany. On July 1, the western economic system absorbed East Germany. With western economic principles dominant in the whole of Germany, the need for a continuing East German government became less and less defensible.

East Berliners wait in line at a Deutsche Bank office for their 100-deutschmark "Welcome Money," November 1989.

With the Kaiser Wilhelm Memorial Church in the background, East Germans shop and stroll through the streets of West Berlin in November 1989.

East German police check East Berliners returning from West Berlin at Potsdamer Platz, a newly opened section of the Berlin Wall.

German political unification still depended on the approval of the four powers that had taken over German sovereignty in 1945. Through the early months of 1990, the United States actively supported the West German government's efforts toward unification. France and Great Britain agreed. By the summer of 1990, the only obstacle seemed to be the Soviet Union, which still had 400,000 troops stationed in East Germany. The Soviet Union insisted that any unified Germany would have to withdraw from NATO, a condition that West Germany and the United States resisted. In July, West German Chancellor Helmut Kohl visited Gorbachev in the Caucasus region of the Soviet Union. After their meeting, Gorbachev accepted German unification and withdrew Soviet objections to membership in NATO for a unified German state.

On September 12, 1990, the four powers that had divided Germany after World War II reached an international accord in what became known as the Two Plus Four Treaty. All powers recognized a new Germany as consisting of the territories of the Federal Republic of Germany, the German Democratic Republic, and greater Berlin. The accord confirmed the permanence of the German frontiers with Poland and the loss of other former German territories as a result of the war. Other provisions restricted the deployment of NATO forces and nuclear weapons in the areas that had been part of East Germany. The Soviet Union agreed to withdraw all of its forces by the end of 1994. On October 1, 1990, the United States, France, Great Britain,

"I remember when the Wall came down at the end of our street and what a significant event that was emotionally. I can recall the large gathering as we pushed the panels down and took our hammers and chisels and broke out sections....

"Initially, it was just a sandy strip that you drove through.... Then they came along and removed the electric wiring.... It quickly became a park, the whole no-man's zone, because it had a big asphalt road running up the length of it, and it was a great place to walk your dog, ride your bike, and whatever. So what had been a killing zone became a recreation area, with kids out there throwing balls and flying Frisbees and kites."

Tom Starbuck, civilian employee, U.S. Army

Vendors began selling Russian military uniforms and pieces of the Berlin Wall.

As sections of the Wall were removed, young Berliners explored areas of the city previously inaccessible to them.

"I was in Berlin after the Wall came down, but before unification—that small period of time. And, of course, I went down to the Brandenburg Gate. I had a very curious reaction to that, because there was a flea market/bazaar set up selling uniform items. At that time I had a son in pilot's training, and I was going to buy him a Russian pilot's hat. I had it in my hand and was bargaining the price down. Then all of a sudden I said, 'I can't do this. I just cannot do this.' You have to have some respect for the military career, even though it is the Russians. And I put the hat down and never bought it."

Colonel Lynn Hansen, U.S. Air Force, retired

1945
1946
1947
1948
1949
1950
1951
1952
1953
1954
1955
1956
1957
1958
1959
1960
1961
1962
1963
1964
1965
1966
1967
1968
1969
1970
1971
1972
1973
1974
1975
1976
1977
1978
1979
1980
1981
1982
1983
1984
1985
1986
1987
1988
1989
1990
1991
1992
1993
1994

and the Soviet Union affirmed that their occupation authority and any residual rights would cease to exist once the two Germanys united.

At one minute after midnight on October 3, 1990, the Federal Republic of Germany became the sole German state and gained complete sovereignty over all the territory of the former East Germany and Berlin. In Berlin, declared once again the capital of Germany, a crowd of over a million turned out to celebrate the raising of the German flag at the old Reichstag building just west of the Brandenburg Gate.

> *"I can remember on the third of October [1990] being able to take the U-Bahn [subway] to Unter den Linden and getting out and proceeding through the Brandenburg Gate with about 3 million of my closest friends. Very orderly. My little, at the time three-year-old, son carried a great big German flag, and the military police had date-stamped it for him. . . . We just sort of moseyed through the Brandenburg Gate and after all those years of coming to Berlin—it's still very emotional.*
>
> *"I served here as a soldier in the late '60s, so I know what it was like to be up along the Fulda Gap. I know what it's like to watch through those layers of barbed wire and the dogs and the minefields and see the guns pointed at you, and to hear the appreciation of those that lived closest to the border [about the American presence]. . . . And then to be there in Berlin."*
>
> *Tom Starbuck, civilian employee, U.S. Army*

Europe on October 3, 1990

176

Berliner Jlluftrirte

Sonderausgabe

Dezember 1989 · DM 7,–
Österreich öS 56,– Schweiz sfr 7,–

Das Volk schreibt Geschichte
Tage, die wir nie vergessen

Revolution in der DDR

Publications chronicled the extraordinary events between November 1989 and October 1990.

Berliner Jlluftrirte

Sonderausgabe

3. Oktober 1990 · DM 7,–
Österreich öS 56,– Schweiz sfr 7,–

Deutschland
Die Stunde der Einheit

Was es kostet,
was es bringt

German Unification and the American Military

German unification changed the basis for the American presence in Berlin. In West Germany, American troops constituted part of the NATO defensive system and remained in the country under the status of forces agreements governing the presence of NATO troops in host nations. In Berlin, by contrast, Americans had always based their troop presence on the four-power status of the city.

When the four powers pledged that the occupation regime would end with the declaration of the unified German state, the occupation authority of the Berlin Command ended. Accordingly, U.S. Commander, Berlin, Major General Raymond Haddock, held a ceremony at Clay Headquarters on October 1, 1990, at which he formally furled the colors of the Berlin Command. Haddock and his successor became simply commanders of the United States Army, Berlin. At the same time, the U.S. Military Liaison Mission ceased its operations and cased its colors. Its mission to monitor the disposition of Soviet forces in East Germany was over.

Col. Richard Naab and Lt. Gen. John Shalikashvili furl the colors at the ceremony inactivating the U.S. Military Liaison Mission, October 1, 1990.

Patch of the Berlin Brigade

Unification and the end of the Cold War changed the role of the Berlin Command. The command began to scale back its operations. In a formal ceremony on June 22, 1990, it deactivated the military police installation at Checkpoint Charlie. Foreign ministers from the United States, France, Great Britain, the Soviet Union, and both Germanys attended, as well as 150 honored guests and 500 representatives of the media. At the end of the ceremony, a crane hoisted the Checkpoint Charlie guardhouse out of the Friedrichstrasse.

Both Germans and Americans on the street for the ceremony expressed a mixture of joy tinged with sadness—sadness that this drama-filled spot would pass into obscurity, and joy that the need for it had disappeared. Soviet Foreign Minister Edward Shevardnadze remarked in his public comments, "One of the emotion-filled pages of Berlin's postwar history is turned. I wish the city of Berlin to become one of the biggest centers of the new system of stability and security in Europe."

The work of the Berlin Command had not ceased with the collapse of the Wall, nor had the closing of Checkpoint Charlie or the inactivation of the command itself ended the American presence in Berlin. When the Wall opened, American military forces responded immediately to the new demands on them. Thousands of refugees flooded into West Berlin. Along with the French and British military contingents, American forces cooperated with city agencies to house, feed, and sustain these people for several months.

The West German government believed that the presence of American and allied troops helped to stabilize the city, so it asked the western powers to remain in Berlin until Soviet troops had completely withdrawn in 1994. Any threat from the Soviet Union seemed unlikely, but the whirlwind pace of change sweeping Eastern Europe dictated prudence.

No longer required to defend Berlin, the U.S. Army's Berlin Brigade quickly reorganized into a light, air-mobile contingency force. It deployed elements to serve in the Persian Gulf War of 1990 and 1991 and to support humanitarian operations in northern Iraq and Turkey, Somalia, and Croatia. Soldiers of the Berlin Brigade also became the first American combat forces to deploy for a United Nations peacekeeping mission. They traveled to Macedonia, a republic of the former Yugoslavia, and remained on duty there in late 1994.

Drawing Down

The Berlin Command's principal mission between 1990 and 1994 was to wrap up its operations within the city. In September 1990, the Berlin Brigade announced the pullout of the 4th Battalion, 502 Infantry, by the following spring. The command held a withdrawal ceremony for the unit on December 14.

The Checkpoint Charlie guardhouse was removed by a crane at a ceremony held June 22, 1990.

"[One thing that] gives the [U.S.] military a very good image in the new states—the military libraries have been dissolved. In ceremonial acts they are donated to cities or to be incorporated into the university library. . . . That's very much appreciated, although, one has to say in all fairness, that doesn't do away with their shortage of books."

Renate Semler, Program Director, Amerika Haus, Berlin

Col. Stephen Bowman leads the color guard at the inactivation of the U.S. Army, 4th Battalion, 502 Infantry, on December 14, 1990.

181

1945
1946
1947
1948
1949
1950
1951
1952
1953
1954
1955
1956
1957
1958
1959
1960
1961
1962
1963
1964
1965
1966
1967
1968
1969
1970
1971
1972
1973
1974
1975
1976
1977
1978
1979
1980
1981
1982
1983
1984
1985
1986
1987
1988
1989
1990
1991
1992
1993
1994

On January 29, 1993, the United States Air Force's 7350th Air Base Group held its inactivation ceremony at Tempelhof air base, ending 48 years of service in Berlin. During the next six months, Air Force personnel turned over various parts of the facility to German governmental bureaus. These organizations—the Bundesgrenzschutz (Federal Border Guard), the Bundesanstalt für Flugsicherung (Federal Institute for Flight Safety), and the Berliner Flughaven Gesellschaft (Berlin Airport Corporation)—increased their use of the facilities as the Air Force withdrew.

Tempelhof never ceased to operate as it progressively changed hands. Most Air Force personnel departed by June 30, 1993. A small contingent of 35 air traffic controllers remained at the Berlin Air Route Traffic Control Center at Tempelhof to work through the summer of 1994.

Former East German refugee Col. Dieter Satz served in Berlin as the U.S. Air Force commander at Tempelhof air base from 1987 to 1990.

As the soldiers and dependents left Berlin, topics of discussion included the future use of facilities in the American sector. Named for Harry S Truman, 33rd president of the United States, Truman Plaza was originally built in the 1950s, then renovated in the late 1970s and 1980s to combine the original free-standing structures into an outdoor mall. Truman Plaza included a post exchange (PX), commissary, bank, laundry, a Burger King, and other community services.

"Truman Plaza, that certainly was an American presence, the American shopping area. It is built in the American style of things . . . the series of shops— strip malls—PX, commissary, and so forth. You don't find that exact character anywhere else in the German community. A statue of Harry S Truman, a statue of George Washington."

Tom Starbuck, civilian employee, U.S. Army

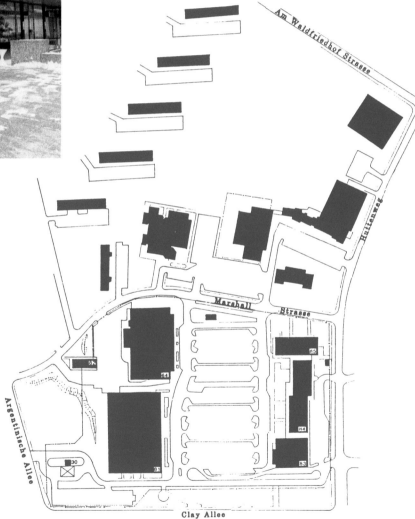

1945
1946
1947
1948
1949
1950
1951
1952
1953
1954
1955
1956
1957
1958
1959
1960
1961
1962
1963
1964
1965
1966
1967
1968
1969
1970
1971
1972
1973
1974
1975
1976
1977
1978
1979
1980
1981
1982
1983
1984
1985
1986
1987
1988
1989
1990
1991
1992
1993
1994

Between the inactivation ceremony at Tempelhof in January 1993 and September 1994, the American military closed 31 facilities in Berlin. These included Andrews Barracks, McNair Barracks, the U.S. Army hospital, and General Lucius D. Clay Headquarters—names and places associated with the presence of U.S. military troops for nearly half a century.

On June 18, 1994, soldiers of the three western allies, the "protecting powers" as they became known in West Berlin, marched down the 17th of June Avenue in a final display of allied military pageantry. It was the 27th and final Allied Forces Day parade, an annual ceremony begun in 1964 to demonstrate allied unity to West Berliners. The parade had been suspended after the Wall came down in 1989, but it was reinstituted for this occasion.

As American forces withdrew from Berlin, enrollment at the Berlin American High School declined.

Andrews Barracks, occupied since 1945 by the U.S. Army, was one of the installations returned to Germany as American military units left Berlin.

Turner Barracks, constructed in 1951 on a wooded site adjacent to the Grünewald, was the home of the U.S. Army, Company F, 40th Armored Regiment, the only tank unit in Berlin and the largest of its kind in the U.S. Army.

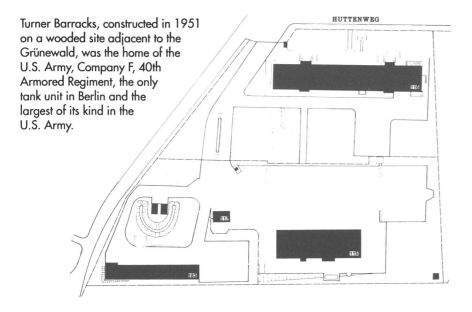

HUTTENWEG

With the troops and the tanks of Company F gone, apartments are empty and grass grows in seams of the pavement in front of the empty maintenance building.

Three weeks later, on July 12, President Bill Clinton visited Berlin, the first visit by an American president since the collapse of the Wall. Clinton visited the German Reichstag building. He and German Chancellor Helmut Kohl walked through the Brandenburg Gate, accompanied only by their wives. Clinton addressed a crowd near the gate, close to where other American presidents had spoken before him. He then attended an afternoon ceremony with the Berlin Brigade where he reviewed the 4,000 troops assembled on the parade grounds of McNair Barracks. When the color guard had furled the brigade colors and slid them into the case, President Clinton took the colors, passed them to the command sergeant major, and commended all the soldiers who had served in Berlin and "who helped bring [the Cold War] to an end."

Drawing the Balance

When the American forces arrived in Berlin in July 1945, they came as conquerors of a Germany ravaged by war and the excesses of hatred that characterized the Nazi era. In 1994, they left as allies of a democratic Germany that had developed new political and economic institutions based on freedom, pluralism, and compromise. American forces departed as friends of the Berliners they had protected for nearly 50 years.

Because of American military troops stationed in Berlin, the city survived as a beacon of freedom and hope in a dreary and repressive world of East German communism. Had the

American troops not been present in 1948, the Soviet blockade could have succeeded in isolating Berlin from contact with the western half of Germany. The costs of breaking the blockade would surely have been high, because the Soviets would have controlled landing strips as well as ground access to the city. Geography was on their side.

Had American forces, in Berlin and in West Germany, not supplied the city during the blockade, it surely would have succumbed to Soviet pressure. West Berlin would not have served as a window of escape from the communist east. No wall would have been erected in 1961, and no wall would have collapsed in 1989. Would Germany have been unified all the same? No one can say, but if unification had occurred, it would have been quite a different Germany and quite a different Berlin from the one which American forces left in 1994.

Just as the American presence influenced the development of Berlin and Germany, Berlin and its people influenced the development of the United States. The interaction is obvious in some ways. Military personnel married Berliners and raised successive generations of German-American children. Soldiers sang German songs at Volksfests, drank beer with Berliners in local bars, and shopped along the Ku-damm. Americans

In the summer of 1991, the German government's restoration of the Brandenburg Gate included removing the Quadriga, the goddess of victory in the four-horse chariot.

President and Mrs. Clinton and Chancellor and Mrs. Kohl walked through the Brandenburg Gate from West to East, July 12, 1994.

By August 1992, the Quadriga had been returned and the gate was reopened to traffic.

1945
1946
1947
1948
1949
1950
1951
1952
1953
1954
1955
1956
1957
1958
1959
1960
1961
1962
1963
1964
1965
1966
1967
1968
1969
1970
1971
1972
1973
1974
1975
1976
1977
1978
1979
1980
1981
1982
1983
1984
1985
1986
1987
1988
1989
1990
1991
1992
1993
1994

lived in a foreign community that welcomed them and appreciated why they were there. Berlin is called the most pro-American city in the world with good reason. For these American soldiers, the Cold War was palpable, the contrasts between communism and capitalism were visible, and the pain of West Berliners separated by the Wall was very real.

These soldiers carried home to the United States an experience of Germany that continued to affect their lives. Many stayed in touch with friends made during their tour. Many retained an interest in German affairs. Most never forgot. It would be difficult to design an educational exchange program that could match these experiences—or replace them.

More subtle than these personal interactions are the ways the American military presence in Berlin contributed to the American public's perceptions of Germany in the Cold War. Americans of a certain age know about the Russian blockade and how the airlift saved West Berlin. The symbolism of the Wall was powerful—on one side freedom, threatened; on the other side oppression, threatening. President Kennedy's assertion, "Ich bin ein Berliner," captivated Americans as well as Berliners. Americans knew that their soldiers were in Berlin, putting their lives on the line. Rare was the suggestion that they abandon their post.

The men and women of the American armed forces serving in Berlin between 1945 and 1994 contributed to a powerful image of the Cold War and to a strikingly positive set of possibili-

ties for the future. By the time American troops departed, Central and Eastern Europe enjoyed an opportunity for economic and political development in freedom and peace unprecedented in their history. A united Germany could call on the strong democratic institutions and political practices developed under the Federal Republic. The new German state was better adapted to the demands of a pluralistic society than any government in Germany's past.

President Clinton's words at the casing of the colors for the Berlin Brigade in July 1994 are a fitting tribute: "With the Cold War over, we gather to honor those Americans who helped bring it to an end. America salutes you. Mission accomplished." American military forces made a crucial contribution. Looking at a united and democratic Germany, at a Cold War ended without cataclysm, at a Berlin once again whole, those who served in the Berlin Command can take enormous pride in that service.

President Clinton addressed a large crowd on the east side of the Brandenburg Gate, July 12, 1994.

Berlin, unified in 1990

Information about Individuals Giving Testimony

The authors recorded interviews with the following individuals. Unless otherwise indicated, the interviews were conducted by both Donita M. Moorhus and Robert P. Grathwol.

Lieutenant Colonel Robert Baldinger, U.S. Army, retired. Served in Berlin as Director of Engineering and Housing, Berlin Command, 1985 to 1988. Interviewed in Hoensbruck, The Netherlands, August 23, 1989.

Klaus Bartels. Berliner, former Commander of the 6941st Guard Battalion (Labor Service). Interviewed in Berlin, Germany, November 25, 1993.

James Bourk. Served in Berlin as an enlisted airman, U.S. Air Force, 1951 to 1954. Interviewed by Donita M. Moorhus by telephone, July 12, 1994.

Louis Brettschneider. Civilian employee of the U.S. Army Corps of Engineers in Europe since 1955. Interviewed in Frankfurt, Germany, January 26 and 30, 1990.

Major General Norman Delbridge, U.S. Army, retired. Served in Berlin as an Army engineer officer, 1947 to 1949. Interviewed in Washington, D.C., February 14, 1990.

Saul Fraint. Civilian employee of the U.S. Army in Europe, 1950 to 1973. Interviewed in Vienna, Austria, August 9, 1990.

Colonel James R. Graham, U.S. Air Force, retired. Served in Berlin as a 1st lieutenant and captain with the 6912th Security Squadron, 1969 to 1973. Interviewed in Washington, D.C., November 10, 1993.

Colonel Lynn M. Hansen, U.S. Air Force, retired. As a commissioned officer, spent 1960 to 1961 in Berlin on a Fulbright scholarship; served on active duty in Berlin assigned to the U.S. Military Liaison Mission as a lieutenant, 1961 to 1963, and as a major, 1971 to 1975. Interviewed at Ramstein Air Base, November 23, 1993.

Daniel Lucas. Served in Berlin as an enlisted soldier, 1977 to 1979. Interviewed by Robert P. Grathwol by telephone, July 30, 1994.

Helga Mellmann. Native Berliner, photographer and archivist for the U.S. Air Forces in Europe at Tempelhof, 1963 to 1993. Interviewed in Berlin, Germany, November 26, 1993.

Renate Semler. Native Berliner, Director of Programs at Amerika Haus, Berlin. Interviewed in Berlin, Germany, November 25, 1993.

Tom Starbuck. Served in Germany in the 1960s as a U.S. Army officer; civilian employee of the U.S. Army Corps of Engineers, 1984 to 1990 and 1992 to present; civilian employee in Directorate of Engineering and Housing, Berlin Command, 1990 to 1992. Interviewed in Frankfurt, Germany, November 19, 1993.

The testimony from **Martin Reuss** was from a personal, unrecorded conversation with the authors. Dr. Reuss was an exchange student at the University of Cologne in 1965, a graduate student at the Free University of Berlin from 1968 to 1969, and a visitor to Berlin in 1992.

The testimony from **Mark Taylor** is from a letter to Helga Mellmann which she shared with the authors.

The testimony from **Colonel H. G. Sheen** is quoted by Earl F. Ziemke in *The U.S. Army in the Occupation of Germany, 1944–1946*, p. 298.

Commanders in Berlin

U.S. Commanders, Berlin		Berlin Brigade Commanders		Tempelhof Base Commanders	
MG Maxwell D. Taylor	31 Aug 49–31 Jan 51	BG Maurice W. Daniel	Jun 50–Jul 53	COL William G. Booth	Jul 1945–Sep 1947
MG Lemuel Mathewson	01 Feb 51–02 Jan 53	BG Charles F. Craig	19 Jul 53–08 Apr 54	COL Henry W. Dorr	Sep 1947–Aug 1948
MG Thomas S. Timbermann	03 Jan 53–04 Aug 54	BG Francis T. Pachler	08 May 54–07 Dec 55	COL Carl Feldman	Aug 1948–Jan 1949
MG George Honnen	05 Aug 54–09 Sep 55	MG Hugh P. Harris	08 Dec 55–30 Sep 56	COL William H. Delacey	Jan 1949–Apr 1949
MG Charles L. Dasher	10 Sep 55–02 Jun 57	BG George T. Duncan	01 Oct 56–01 Sep 58	COL John E. Barr	Apr 1949–Jul 1951
MG Barksdale Hamlett	03 Jun 57–14 Dec 59	BG Charles S. D'Orsa	05 Sep 58–15 Jan 60	COL John V. Hart	Jul 1951–Mar 1953
MG Ralph M. Osborne	15 Dec 59–04 May 61	BG Charles E. Johnson III	15 Jan 60–30 Jul 61	COL Roy L. Jones	Mar 1953–Dec 1954
MG Albert Watson II	05 May 61–02 Jan 63	BG Frederick O. Hartel	30 Jul 61–05 Jul 64	COL Wesley H. Vernon	Dec 1954–Aug 1956
MG James K. Polk	02 Jan 63–31 Aug 64	BG John A. Hay, Jr.	05 Jul 64–02 Aug 66	COL Rex W. Beach	Aug 1956–May 1959
MG John F. Franklin, Jr.	01 Sep 64–03 Jun 67	BG James L. Baldwin	02 Sep 66–19 Oct 67	COL Edward C. Tates	May 1959–Jul 1960
MG Robert G. Fergusson	03 Jun 67–28 Feb 70	BG Samuel McC. Goodwin	18 Nov 67–31 Oct 69	COL Kenneth L. Glassburn	Jul 1960–Jul 1963
MG George M. Seignious II	28 Feb 70–12 May 71	BG Harold I. Hayward	08 Nov 69–10 Jul 71	COL Paul H. Kenney	Aug 1963–Aug 1965
MG William W. Cobb	12 May 71–10 Jun 74	BG Raymond O. Miller	Jul 71–Feb 73	COL Joseph D. White	Aug 1965–Jul 1966
MG Sam S. Walker	10 Jun 74–11 Aug 75	BG Robert D. Stevenson	03 Mar 73–08 Aug 74	COL Thomas A. Personett	Jul 1966–Jul 1968
MG Joseph C. McDonough	11 Aug 75–07 Jun 78	MG R. Dean Tice	09 Sep 74–11 Jun 76	COL Clark A. Tate	Jul 1968–Dec 1969
MG Calvert P. Benedict	07 Jun 78–05 Jul 81	BG Walter E. Adams	11 Jun 76–25 Aug 78	COL David B. Smith	Dec 1969–Feb 1970
MG James G. Boatner	05 Jul 81–27 Jun 84	BG William C. Moore	25 Aug 78–01 Aug 80	COL Gail S. Halvorsen	Feb 1970–Feb 1974
MG John H. Mitchell	27 Jun 84–01 Jun 88	BG John E. Rogers	01 Aug 80–17 Nov 81	COL Mayron G. Smith	Feb 1974–Jul 1976
MG Raymond E. Haddock	01 Jun 88–03 Oct 90	MG Leroy N. Suddath, Jr.	17 Nov 81–25 Jul 84	COL Donald W. Lajeunesse	Jul 1976–Jun 1979
		MG Thomas N. Griffin, Jr.	25 Jul 84–03 Jun 86	COL Vernon L. Frye	Jun 1979–Jul 1981
		MG Jack D. Woodall	03 Jun 86–19 Aug 87	COL Gary E. Spohn	Jul 1981–May 1984
		MG C. G. Marsh	19 Aug 87–16 Nov 89	COL Lonnie R. Spivey	Jun 1984–Jun 1987
		MG Sidney Shachnow	15 Dec 89–14 Aug 91	COL Dieter W. Satz	Jun 1987–Jun 1990
		BG Walter H. Yates	14 Aug 91–18 Sep 92	COL Joseph W. Sellmann	Jun 1990–Feb 1991
		COL Jimmy Banks	19 Sep 92–12 Jul 94	COL Gary L. Lindner	Feb 1991–Jun 1993

Acronyms

AACS	Army Airways Communications System		KPD	Communist Party of Germany (German)
AAFES	Army and Air Force Exchange Service		MATS	Military Air Transport Service
AFN	Armed Forces Network		MPs	Military Police
BRD	Federal Republic of Germany (German)		NATO	North Atlantic Treaty Organization
CARE	Cooperative for American Relief to Everywhere		NAVAIDS	Navigational Aids
DPs	Displaced Persons		OMGUS	Office of Military Government, United States
ERP	European Recovery Program		PXs	Post Exchanges
EUCOM	European Command		RIAS	Radio in the American Sector
FRG	Federal Republic of Germany		SBZ	Soviet Zone of Occupation (German)
GDR	German Democratic Republic		SED	Social Unity Party of Germany (German)
GIs	Members of the U.S. Armed Forces, especially enlisted personnel. Term derived from "Government Issue."		SPD	Social Democratic Party (German)
			TCA	Tempelhof Central Airport
GYA	German Youth Activity		USAFE	United States Air Forces in Europe
HICOG	High Commission for Germany		USCOB	United States Commander, Berlin
INF	Intermediate-Range Nuclear Forces		USFET	United States Forces, European Theater
JG	Junior Grade		USMLM	United States Military Liaison Mission

Photographs and Illustrative Material

The following United States government offices provided photographs and illustrations:

Library of Congress
U.S. Air Force
U.S. Air Forces in Europe, Office of History
U.S. Army, Berlin
    Directorate of Engineering and Housing
    Office of Plans, Training, Mobilization, and Security
U.S. Army Corps of Engineers, Headquarters, Office of History
U.S. Army, Europe, Office of History
U.S. Army Military History Institute

U.S. Department of Defense
    Public Affairs Office
    Still Media Depository
The White House, Office of Photography

The following individuals contributed photographs and memorabilia from personal collections:

Klaus P. Bartels, James Bourk, Stephen L. Bowman, James and Lani Graham, Robert P. Grathwol, Daniel C. Lucas, Helga Th. Mellmann, Richard Naab, Martin Reuss, Paul K. Walker, Douglas J. Wilson, and Kenneth Wunsche.

Some of the photographs supplied for this manuscript from the sources listed originated from the Landesbildstelle in Berlin.

Suggested Readings on Berlin and Germany

Bark, Dennis L., and David R. Gress. *A History of West Germany*, 2 vols. Oxford University Press, 1989.

Clay, Lucius D. *Decision in Germany*. Doubleday, 1950 (reprinted in 1970 by Greenwood Press).

Clay, Lucius D. *The Papers of Lucius D. Clay: Germany, 1945-1949*; 2 vols. Jean Edward Smith, Editor. Books on Demand, University Microfilms International.

Francisco, Ronald, and Richard L. Merritt. *Berlin Between Two Worlds*. Westview Press, 1985.

Friedrich, Otto. *Before the Deluge: A Portrait of Berlin in the 1920s*. Harper & Row, 1972.

Gavin, James M. *On to Berlin*. Viking Press, 1978.

Halvorsen, Gail S. *Berlin Candy Bomber*. Horizon Publishers & Distributors, Inc., 1990.

Howley, Frank. *Berlin Command*. Putnam, 1950.

Liang, Hsi-Huey. *Berlin Before the Wall: A Foreign Student's Diary with Sketches*. Routledge, 1990.

Maginnis, Major General John J. *Military Government Journal*. Robert A. Hart, Editor. University of Massachusetts Press, 1971.

Smith, Jean Edward. *Lucius D. Clay: An American Life*. Henry Holt & Co., 1990.

Turner, Henry Ashby, Jr. *Germany from Partition to Reunification*. Yale University Press, 1992.

Ziemke, Earl F. *The U.S. Army in the Occupation of Germany, 1944-1946*. U.S. Army Center of Military History, 1975.

Index

ISBN 0-16-045272-4